# THE LEGO® ARCHITECT

# TOM ALPHIN

SAN FRANCISCO

**The LEGO® Architect.** Copyright © 2015 by Tom Alphin.

Printed in Korea

Fourth Printing

19 18 17 16      4 5 6 7 8 9

ISBN-10: 1-59327-613-3
ISBN-13: 978-1-59327-613-3

Publisher: William Pollock
Production Editor: Alison Law
Cover and Interior Design: Beth Middleworth
Cover Model: UNITÉ D'HABITATION, designed by Ken Parel-Sewell and built by Dan Madryga
Cover Photograph: Dean Lavenson
Developmental Editor: Tyler Ortman
Copyeditor: Rachel Monaghan
Proofreader: Emelie Burnette
Indexing: BIM Indexing & Proofreading Services

For information on distribution, translations, or bulk sales, please contact No Starch Press, Inc. directly:

No Starch Press, Inc.
245 8th Street, San Francisco, CA 94103
phone: 415.863.9900; info@nostarch.com; www.nostarch.com

Library of Congress Cataloging-in-Publication Data
Alphin, Tom.
  The LEGO architect / by Tom Alphin.
      pages cm
  Includes bibliographical references.
  Summary: "Uses LEGO models to explore Neoclassical, Art Deco, Brutalist, Modernist, and other architectural styles. Each chapter includes a discussion of the architectural movement, photographs of famous real-life buildings, and a gallery of LEGO models, with step-by-step building instructions." -- Provided by publisher.
  ISBN 978-1-59327-613-3 -- ISBN 1-59327-613-3
  1. Architectural models. 2. Architecture, Modern--Themes, motives. 3. LEGO toys. I. Title.
  NA2790.A56 2015
  724--dc23
                         2015017603

# TABLE OF CONTENTS

# PREFACE

LEGO always had its roots in architecture—after all, the little plastic pieces are called bricks! In this book, you will learn about real-life architecture by building it with LEGO. Photos of real buildings and amazing LEGO models created by talented artists from around the world will inspire you, and you'll learn about the history of architecture along the way.

This book grew from my own architectural explorations with LEGO. I was inspired by the LEGO Architecture Studio set, which includes over 1000 white and clear LEGO bricks but absolutely no instructions. This set forces you to design your own models, which is a great challenge that I hope you are inspired to try. By learning about influential architectural styles, I hope that you will be able to better appreciate the buildings in your own city and find inspiration for your own LEGO architecture creations.

While the chapters in this book are neatly organized into distinct styles, the real world is much more complicated. Architects are constantly blending old and new ideas to create innovative designs, and new styles are born when buildings by different architects converge on a new approach. Over time, architectural styles fall out fashion, and they sometimes reappear years later. By combining your favorite elements from different styles, you can create a unique style of your own.

## ABOUT THE BUILDING INSTRUCTIONS

The building instructions in this book use only white and clear bricks. This keeps the instructions simple and allows us to focus on the key features that define each style. Don't feel like you need to follow the directions literally—use the colors you already have and substitute different parts as needed. At the beginning of each set of instructions, part numbers are listed to help you order additional bricks online if you need them. Many of the models in this book can be built using just the parts from the LEGO Architecture Studio set, and the rest use fairly common parts that you might already have.

## ACKNOWLEDGMENTS

This book celebrates the vibrant community of artists around the world who choose LEGO as their medium. I was amazed by the enthusiastic response from LEGO builders when I asked to include their work. Thank you to the LEGO artists featured in this book, my beta readers, SEALUG, and the community as a whole.

This book is dedicated to my family. To my parents, for the gifts of curiosity, travel, and a lot of LEGO sets. To Amy, for patience as I filled our house with sharp plastic bricks and for her unwavering love of teaching and learning, which inspires me every day.

Visit *http://nostarch.com/legoarchitect* for a list of the LEGO bricks needed for every model in the book. While you're there, you can also get bonus content like building instructions for this Neoclassical monument.

# A BRIEF HISTORY OF ARCHITECTURE

The architectural styles explored in this book represent some of the most important in the modern era (the last 500 years), with a focus on Western architectural styles common in Europe and North America. That said, you will also see how Asian architecture influenced the Prairie and Postmodern styles, and how Egyptian and Mesoamerican architecture influenced Art Deco.

Looking back to the early history of architecture, we have limited information because little remains of early homes built of perishable natural materials like wood, leather, and clay. We do get a glimpse of early architectural history by looking at the remains of 5,000-year-old stone houses in Northern Scotland, the stone rings at Stonehenge, the cliff dwellings at Mesa Verde, and the great pyramids of Egypt.

The Egyptians were some of the first to employ columns in their buildings, but the Greeks are more famous for using long rows of slender columns in their temples, such as the famous Parthenon in Athens (438 BCE). The Romans expanded on the clean, classical forms of Greek architecture while pushing the limits of architecture and engineering much further. They embraced the structural potential of arches in everything from aqueducts and bridges to the Coliseum (80 CE). The Romans were also the first to master the use of concrete, most famously with the domed roof of the Pantheon, which has been standing since 126 CE and is still the largest unreinforced concrete dome in the world.

The next major revolution in architectural forms came when architects invented the pointed, or Gothic, arch as a way to create brightly lit spaces with stone and glass. Tall windows filled with brightly colored stained glass allowed more light into the great cathedrals built during this period. Flying buttresses made it possible for architects to build even bigger cathedrals, as the buttresses kept the walls from crumpling under the force of the massive arches, as seen in the iconic Cathédrale Notre-Dame de Paris (1163–1345 CE). The decadence of Gothic architecture evolved into increasingly decorated styles, such as the ornate Baroque and fussy Rococo styles that preceded the Neoclassical period.

It is here that our book begins, as we follow a rapid progression of architectural styles that were inspired by the advent of new materials, emerging technologies, and social pressures. We will see how Neoclassical architects found inspiration in the past; how the open prairie inspired its own style; how a period of wealth and flamboyance was reflected in the Art Deco style; how new materials and technology made Modernism possible; how economic pressures led Modernism to evolve into Brutalism; how a disdain for boring minimalist designs gave rise to Postmodernism; and how computer modeling ushered in creative High-Tech designs.

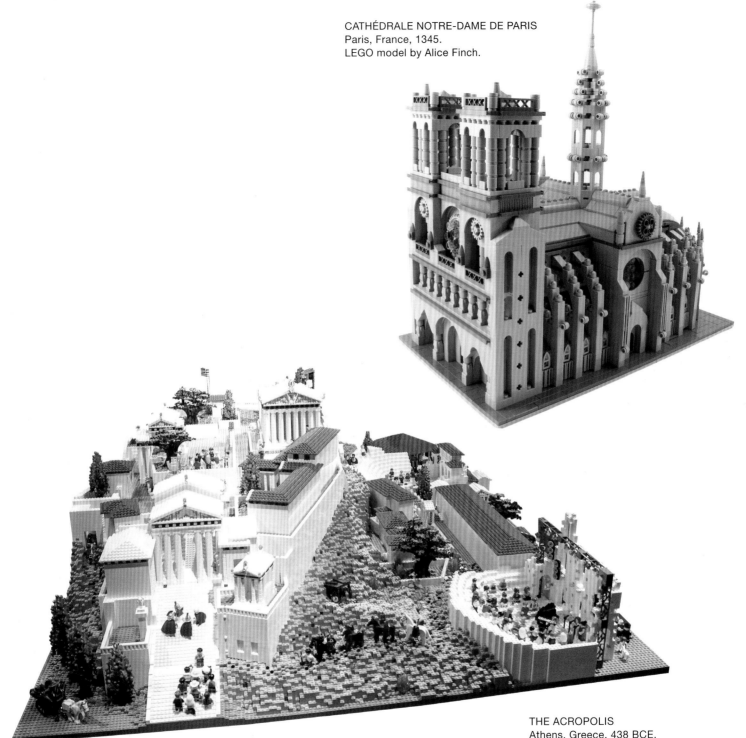

CATHÉDRALE NOTRE-DAME DE PARIS
Paris, France, 1345.
LEGO model by Alice Finch.

THE ACROPOLIS
Athens, Greece, 438 BCE.
LEGO model by Ryan McNaught.

# NEOCLASSICAL

Neoclassical architecture emerged during a period of renewed interest in ancient Greek and Roman visual art, design, and literature. The style emphasizes symmetry and simplicity. Many Neoclassical buildings feature tall columns capped with a triangular pediment and a large domed roof, similar to the ancient Roman Pantheon.

THE ROTUNDA, UNIVERSITY OF VIRGINIA
Charlottesville, Virginia, 1826,
Thomas Jefferson.

**WHITE HOUSE**
Washington, DC, 1800,
James Hoban.

**VILLA EMO**
Fanzolo di Vedelago, Italy, 1565,
Andrea Palladio.

**ARC DE TRIOMPHE**
Paris, France, 1836,
Jean Chalgrin and Louis-Étienne Héricart de Thury.

**ROYAL SALTWORKS**
Arc-et-Senans, France, 1775,
Claude-Nicolas Ledoux.

The mainstream Neoclassical movement of the mid-18th century was preceded by the works of Andrea Palladio, an Italian architect whose 1570 treatise, *I Quattro Libri dell'Architettura* (*The Four Books of Architecture*), cataloged the key features of classical Greek and Roman architecture. Palladio reverse-engineered designs from antiquity to create detailed guidelines governing the correct size and position of columns, pediments, and other classical forms. Neoclassical buildings that adhere closely to these principles are described as *Palladian*.

Palladio's strict interpretation of classical architecture was ahead of its time in a period when most European architects were exploring the increasingly decorative Baroque and Rococo styles. While loosely based on classical forms and elements, Baroque architecture often includes exteriors with dramatic facades, indiscriminate use of columns, and interiors lavishly decorated with intricately carved plaster and frescoes. It wasn't until the 1700s that the Baroque style saw serious criticism, when several books condemning its decadence were published. In his 1715 book, *Vitruvius*

## MATERIALS

The primary material used in Neoclassical architecture is carved stone, which is used for walls and columns. Roofing materials are varied but can include shingles, terra-cotta, or metal.

Neoclassical homes are often constructed from lower-cost materials such as brick, which is sometimes covered with stucco and painted a neutral color.

VILLA LA ROTONDA
Vicenza, Italy, 1590,
Andrea Palladio and Vincenzo Scamozzi.

BRANDENBURG GATE
Berlin, Germany, 1791,
Carl Gotthard Langhans.

## LEGO BRICKS

 Round bricks or bars can be used for columns, depending on the scale of your model.

 Arches can be used in designs modeled on Roman tradition.

 Slopes can be used for steep roofs.

 Hemispheres and other curved parts can be used for a domed roof.

*Britannicus*, Colen Campbell challenged the leading Baroque architect, writing, "How wildly Extravagant are the designs of Borromini . . . where the Parts are without Proportion . . . excessive Ornaments without Grace, and the whole without Symmetry?"

By 1750, a new generation of architects and patrons were drawn back to classical styles by these newly published books and their own experiences visiting ancient buildings and ruins. It had become common for well-educated young men to take "grand tours" of Europe, where they saw the great works of Roman antiquity.

This renewed interest in classical styles gave rise to a grand civic architecture throughout Europe that could compete with medieval-era Gothic cathedrals both in scale and social significance. Principal among the Neoclassical style's proponents was French architect Claude-Nicolas Ledoux, whose design for the Royal Saltworks (1775) features unique rusticated columns and classical proportions.

Neoclassical architecture also crossed the Atlantic to the United States. The Roman Republic influenced not only the government of the new democracy, but also its architectural language. Founding father Thomas Jefferson's interest in architecture and his reverence for Palladio is evident in his Rotunda (1826) at the University of Virginia. With Jefferson's support, Neoclassical architecture became the preferred style for federal buildings such as the United States Capitol Building (1793), the White House (1800), and many other iconic monuments in Washington, DC. Neoclassical architecture is still used today in monuments, government buildings, and universities around the world.

## NEOCLASSICAL IN LEGO

LEGO lends itself well to Neoclassical design, as the style tends to be rectangular, strictly symmetrical, and composed of design elements that are easily matched to basic LEGO bricks. The style is characterized by a relatively small degree of ornamentation, especially when compared to the Baroque era that preceded it. This means there aren't as many small details you need to re-create. The biggest challenges are often the massive domes and the gently sloping roofline of pediments, although this chapter includes building instructions for creating both.

**LEGO COLORS**

White

Light bluish grey

Dark bluish grey

Tan

Dark tan

Trans clear

UNITED STATES CAPITOL BUILDING,
Washington, DC, 1793,
William Thornton et al.

# NEOCLASSICAL
# LEGO MODELS

MENIN GATE
Ypres, Belgium, 1927, Reginald Blomfield.
LEGO model by Jan Vanden Berghe.

NEW YORK STOCK EXCHANGE
New York City, New York, 1903, George B. Post.
LEGO model by Sean Kenney.

TO THE ARMIES
OF THE BRITISH EMPIRE
WHO STOOD HERE
FROM 1914 TO 1918
AND TO THOSE OF THEIR DEAD
WHO HAVE NO KNOWN GRAVE

ST PAUL'S CATHEDRAL
London, United Kingdom, 1708, Sir Christopher Wren.
LEGO model by Alex Mallinson.

**ROYAL ALBERT HALL OF ARTS AND SCIENCES**
London, United Kingdom, 1871, Captain Francis Fowke
and Major-General Henry Y.D. Scott, Royal Engineers.
LEGO model by Phil Raines and Deborah Hope.

**VILLA LA ROTONDA**
Vicenza, Italy, 1590,
Andrea Palladio and Vincenzo Scamozzi.
LEGO model by Ferenc Szőke.

MONTICELLO
Charlottesville, Virginia, 1772,
Thomas Jefferson.

# DOMED BUILDING

This model includes many iconic elements of Neoclassical architecture, including a prominent domed roof.

The overall shape is similar to Thomas Jefferson's design for Monticello. This design could be described as Palladian, as it is strictly symmetrical and includes both columns and a pediment.

Domed roof

Triangular pediment

Rustication

Even number of columns

| | | | | | | | | |
|---|---|---|---|---|---|---|---|---|
| 8x | 14x | 3x | 2x | 2x | 16x | 4x | 4x | |
| 3070 | 3069 | 6636 | 4162 | 3068 | 54200 | 3039 | 3045 | |

| | | | | | | | | | | |
|---|---|---|---|---|---|---|---|---|---|---|
| 40x | 16x | 18x | 11x | 12x | 4x | 16x | 6x | 1x | 12x | 4x |
| 3794 | 3024 | 3023 | 3623 | 3710 | 3666 | 2420 | 3022 | 3020 | 4070 | 30414 |

| | | | | | | | | | |
|---|---|---|---|---|---|---|---|---|---|
| 15x | 8x | 6x | 3x | 6x | 2x | 4x | 6x | 4x | 4x |
| 3062a | 3005 | 3622 | 3008 | 2357 | 2456 | 6231 | 30413 | 4490 | 3659 |

| | | | | | |
|---|---|---|---|---|---|
| 4x | 5x | 2x | 3x | 2x | 1x |
| 3031 | 3032 | 3035 | 3036 | 3958 | 41539 |

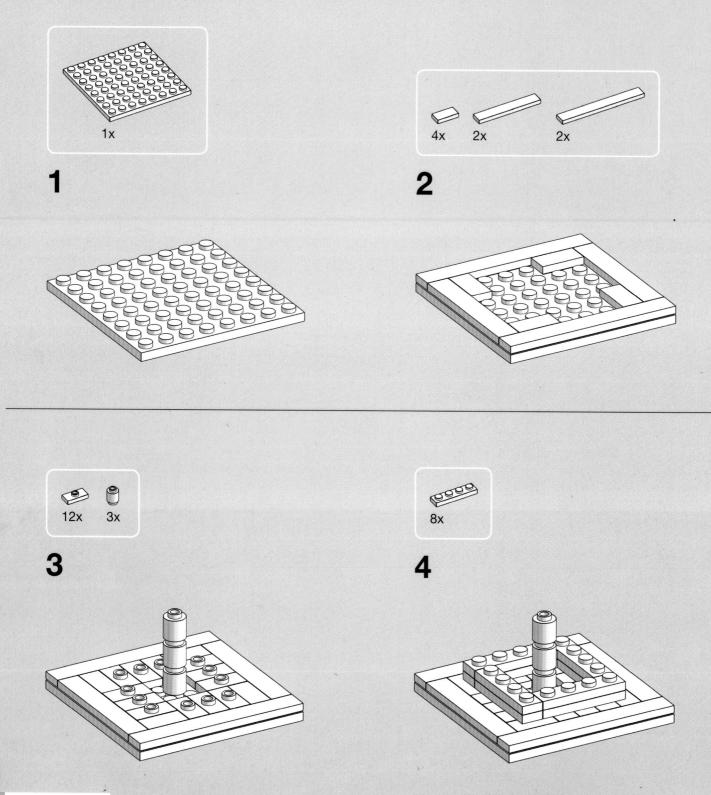

1

1x

2

4x    2x    2x

3

12x    3x

4

8x

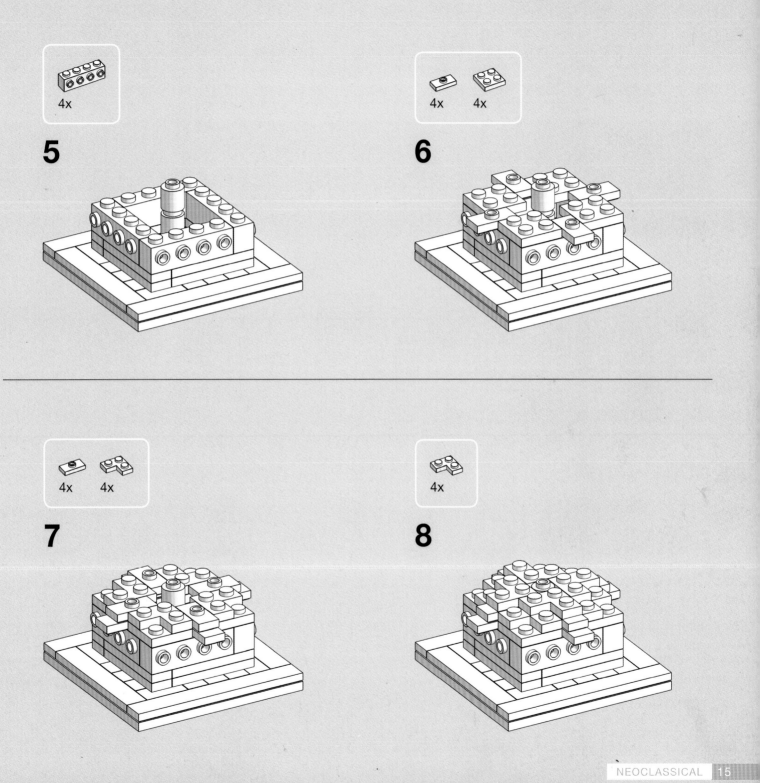

**5**

**6**

4x

4x  4x

**7**

**8**

4x  4x

4x

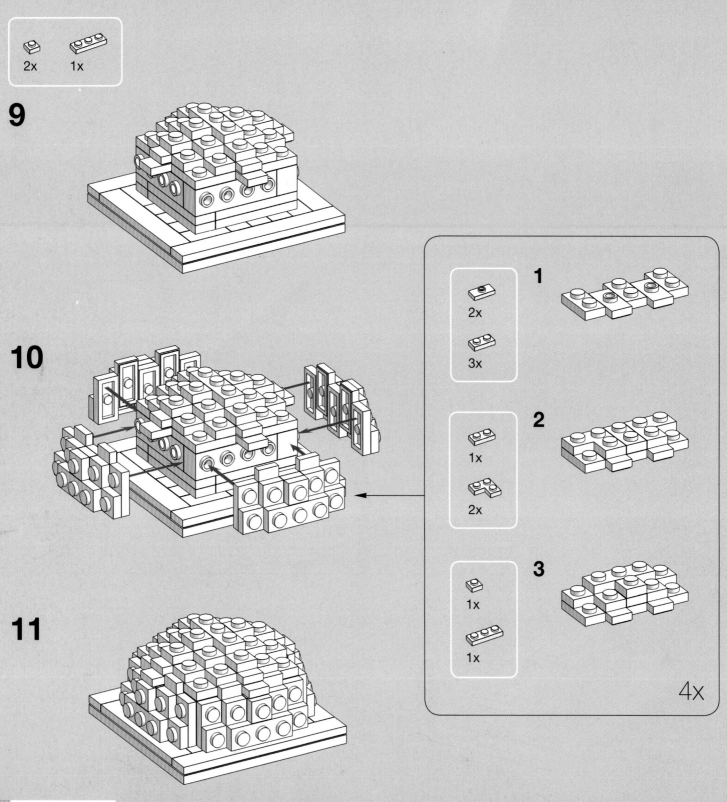

**9**

**10**

1

2x

3x

**1**

**2**

1x

2x

**3**

1x

1x

4x

**11**

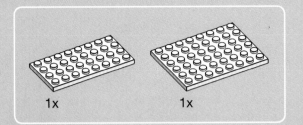

**12**

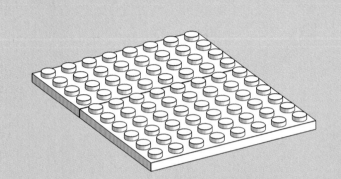

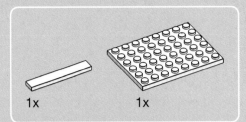

**13**

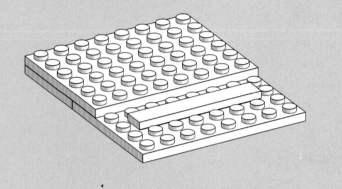

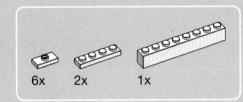

**14**

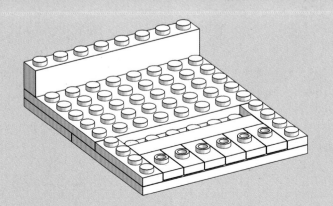

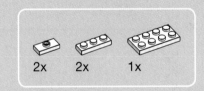

**15**

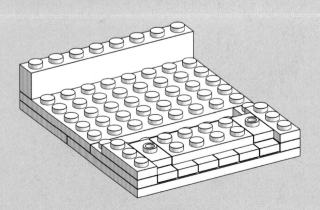

**16**

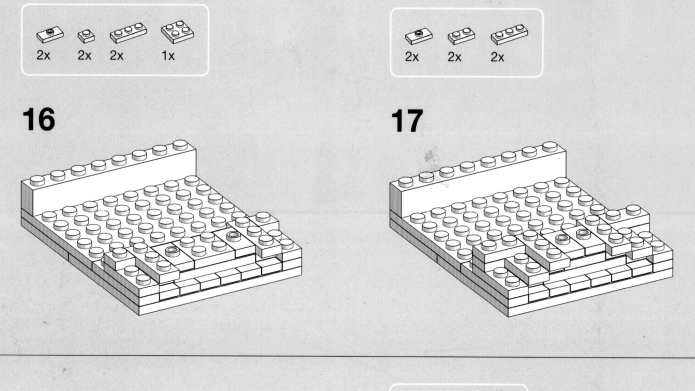

**17**

**18**

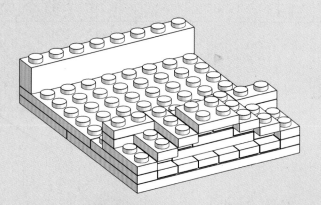

**19**

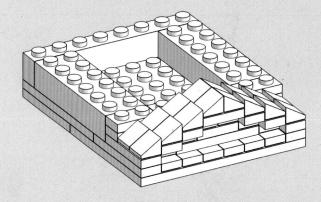

**20**

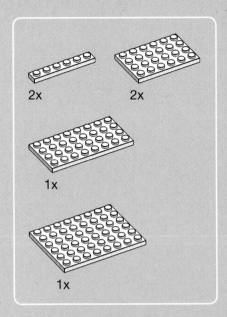

2x

2x

1x

1x

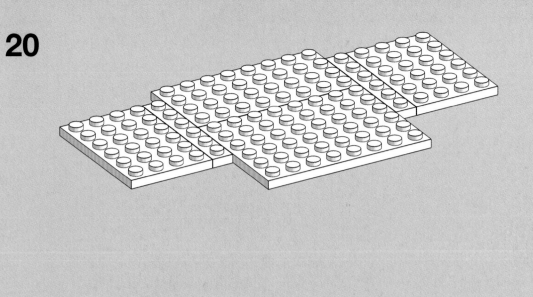

**21**

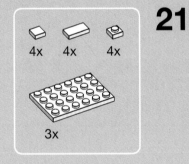

4x 4x 4x

3x

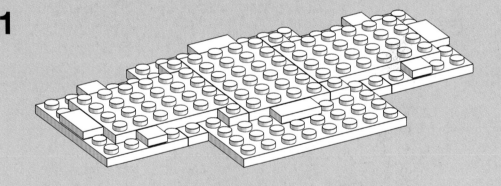

**22**

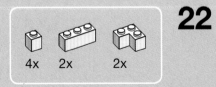

4x 2x 2x

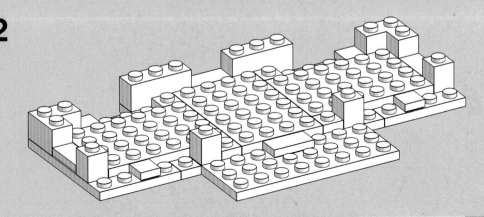

**23**

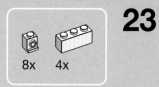 8x 4x

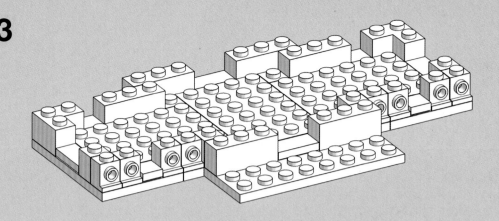

**24**

 4x 4x

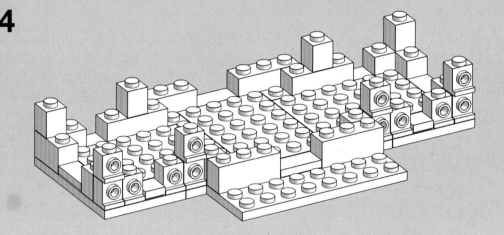

**25**

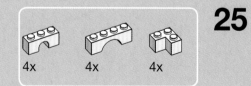 4x 4x 4x

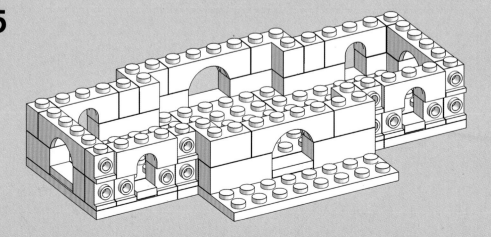

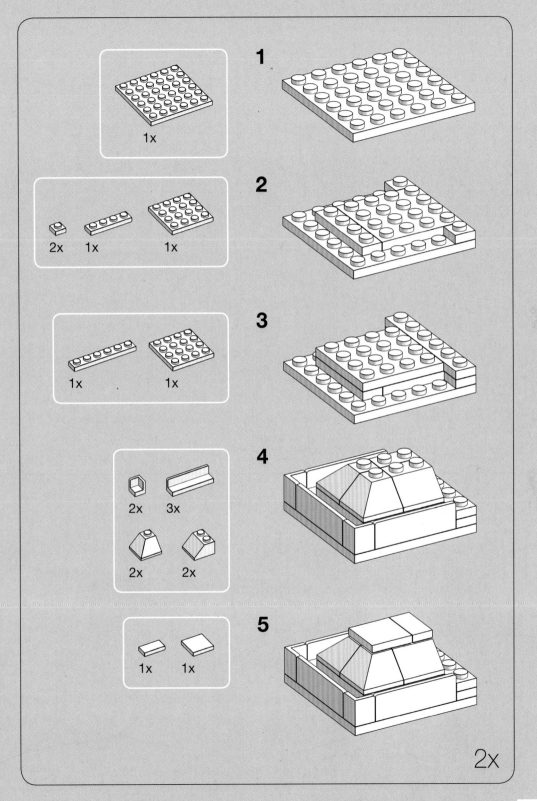

1

1x

2

2x  1x  1x

3

1x  1x

4

2x  3x

2x  2x

5

1x  1x

2x

**26**

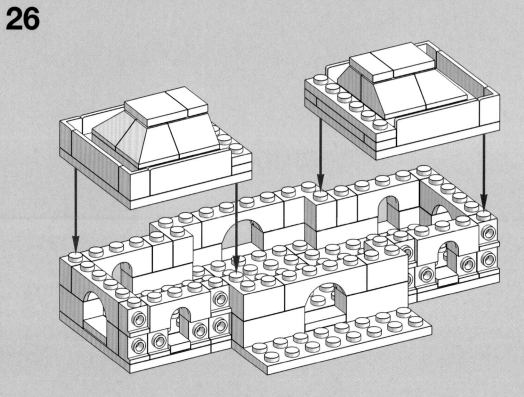

**27**

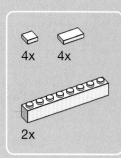

4x    4x

2x

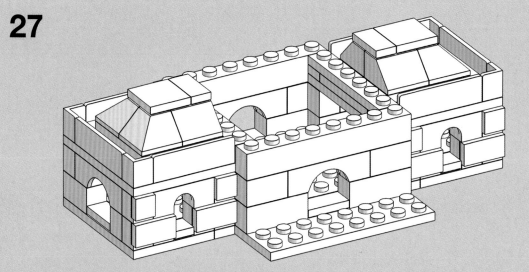

**28**

12x

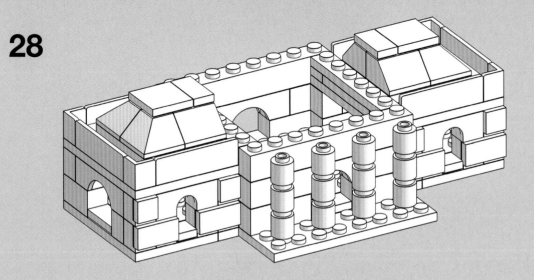

**29**

TALIESIN III
Spring Green, Wisconsin, 1925,
Frank Lloyd Wright.

# PRAIRIE

The seemingly limitless expanses of the American West inspired a new architectural style, which emphasizes horizontal lines, open floor plans, and a connection with nature. This new Prairie style was pioneered by Chicago architect Frank Lloyd Wright, but many other architects designed buildings in the style as it gained popularity within the Midwest and beyond.

GAMBLE HOUSE
Pasadena, California, 1908,
Greene & Greene.

HAROLD C. BRADLEY HOUSE
Madison, Wisconsin, 1909,
Louis Sullivan and George Grant Elmslie.

Frank Lloyd Wright began his career working in the office of Louis Sullivan, whose office buildings were an early precursor to Modernism. Wright left Sullivan's office to design comfortable homes in the suburbs of Chicago, creating the Prairie style.

The Prairie style was inspired by the Arts and Crafts movement, which celebrated traditional handcrafted construction using natural materials as a reaction against industrialization. The Arts and Crafts style was popular in the 1890s in Britain but is also found in the United States—for example, the exquisite Gamble House (1908) in Pasadena, California. The Prairie style was also influenced by the open floor plans of traditional Japanese architecture.

Wright's Prairie homes include the Robie House (1909), a massive rectangular home executed with precision brickwork and interior details. By contrast, Taliesin (1911, 1925), the private retreat Wright built for himself in Wisconsin, is a rambling complex of loosely coupled spaces built near the top of a hill where its occupants could enjoy the panoramic views. A signature design element in Wright's homes is a hidden entrance with a low ceiling that gives a compressed, almost claustrophobic feeling, followed by an expansive space beyond that welcomes guests into the home.

## MATERIALS

Prairie architects prefer natural materials like wood, tinted stucco, or brick. When budgets were limited, rough concrete or stucco was used. Gently sloping shingled roofs with broad overhanging eaves are common.

Another iconic element of the Prairie style is the use of intricate leaded-glass windows. This is especially common in doors, but some homes have leaded glass in every window.

WILLIAM H. EMERY JR. HOUSE
Elmhurst, Illinois, 1903,
Walter Burley Griffin.

ROBIE HOUSE
Hyde Park, Illinois, 1909,
Frank Lloyd Wright.

IMPERIAL HOTEL
Tokyo, Japan, 1923,
Frank Lloyd Wright.

## LEGO BRICKS

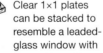 1×2 plates allow you to re-create a detailed brick wall.

 Clear 1×1 plates can be stacked to resemble a leaded-glass window with geometric patterns.

 Tiles allow you to create uninterrupted horizontal surfaces.

 Hinges can be used to create a pitched roof.

Wright's contemporaries took the Prairie style in different directions, and their collective work is sometimes known as the *Prairie School*. Homes by Louis Sullivan and George Elmslie tend to be taller and have steeper pitched roofs, as in the Harold C. Bradley House (1909). Walter Burley Griffin designed buildings with bold, decorative lines, such as the William H. Emery Jr. House (1903). Griffin met his future wife, Marion Mahony, who was a talented draftsman, while they were both working in Wright's office. The couple collaborated on projects for the rest of their lives.

Wright's fascination with Japanese architecture helped him earn a prestigious

commission to build the grand new Imperial Hotel (1923) in Tokyo. Most Western architects working in Japan at the time ignored local traditions, but Wright combined elements of traditional Japanese architecture with the Prairie style to create a modern, uniquely Japanese look. Wright completed several projects in Japan, where his style remained popular, with local architects copying it to varying degrees of success. Arata Endo, Wright's assistant on the Imperial Hotel, went on to create spirited Wrightian works of his own design.

By the 1920s, both Wright and his Prairie style had fallen out of favor. After 10 years with few completed buildings, Wright reemerged as a Modernist with his design for Fallingwater (1937), a modern home that preserved the continuous open spaces he had perfected in his Prairie period.

It was in this period that Wright developed his "Usonian" system of economical, modern homes built out of prefabricated components. He hoped that every American could afford a well-designed home, but only a poor facsimile of his ideas reached the mainstream, as the ranch-style homes of the 1950s and 1960s. The most lasting legacy of the Prairie style is the reinvention of residential interiors as open spaces for cooking, living, and dining.

## PRAIRIE IN LEGO

Prairie is a popular style to re-create with LEGO due to Frank Lloyd Wright's celebrity and the fact that many Prairie homes can be built with a modest collection of common bricks. A 1×2 LEGO plate has the same proportions as the slender Roman bricks used in many Prairie buildings, so you can build a detailed brick home using a large number of dark red or orange plates. The gently sloping roofs can present a challenge because sloped LEGO bricks are too steep. Many builders approximate a Prairie-style roof by stacking LEGO plates, or create a pitched roof using hinges.

## LEGO COLORS

- White
- Light bluish grey
- Medium dark flesh
- Dark red
- Reddish brown
- Tan
- Dark tan
- Olive green
- Trans clear

TALIESIN WEST
Scottsdale, Arizona, 1937,
Frank Lloyd Wright.

# PRAIRIE LEGO MODELS

**WINGSPREAD**
Wind Point, Wisconsin, 1939, Frank Lloyd Wright.
LEGO model by Jameson Gagnepain.

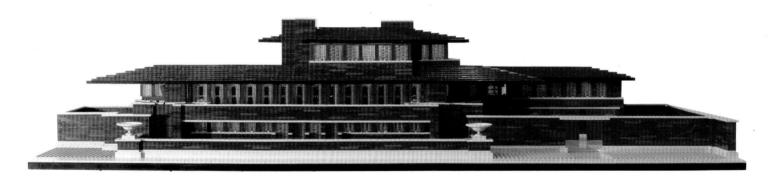

**ROBIE HOUSE**
Hyde Park, Illinois, 1909, Frank Lloyd Wright.
LEGO model by Chris Eyerly.

UNITY TEMPLE
Oak Park, Illinois, 1908, Frank Lloyd Wright.
LEGO model by Grant W. Scholbrock.

GAMBLE HOUSE
Pasadena, California, 1908, Greene & Greene.
LEGO model by Grant W. Scholbrock.

TALIESIN WEST
Scottsdale, Arizona, 1937, Frank Lloyd Wright.
LEGO model by Adam Reed Tucker.

# PRAIRIE HOUSE

This model is based loosely on Willits House (1901) by Frank Lloyd Wright. Many people consider this to be his first great Prairie-style home. The model includes iconic features of Prairie architecture, such as a private patio, a roof with broad eaves, and exaggerated horizontal lines.

This model is designed to be opened, revealing an open floor plan oriented around the hearth.

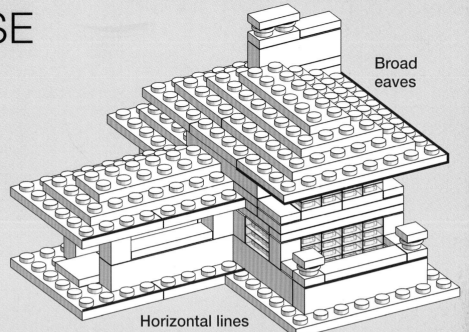

Broad eaves

Horizontal lines

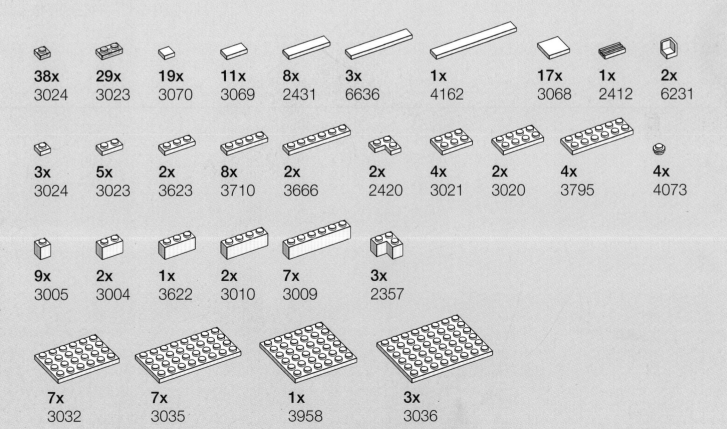

| | | | | | | | | | |
|---|---|---|---|---|---|---|---|---|---|
| **38x** 3024 | **29x** 3023 | **19x** 3070 | **11x** 3069 | **8x** 2431 | **3x** 6636 | **1x** 4162 | **17x** 3068 | **1x** 2412 | **2x** 6231 |
| **3x** 3024 | **5x** 3023 | **2x** 3623 | **8x** 3710 | **2x** 3666 | **2x** 2420 | **4x** 3021 | **2x** 3020 | **4x** 3795 | **4x** 4073 |
| **9x** 3005 | **2x** 3004 | **1x** 3622 | **2x** 3010 | **7x** 3009 | **3x** 2357 | | | | |
| **7x** 3032 | **7x** 3035 | **1x** 3958 | **3x** 3036 | | | | | | |

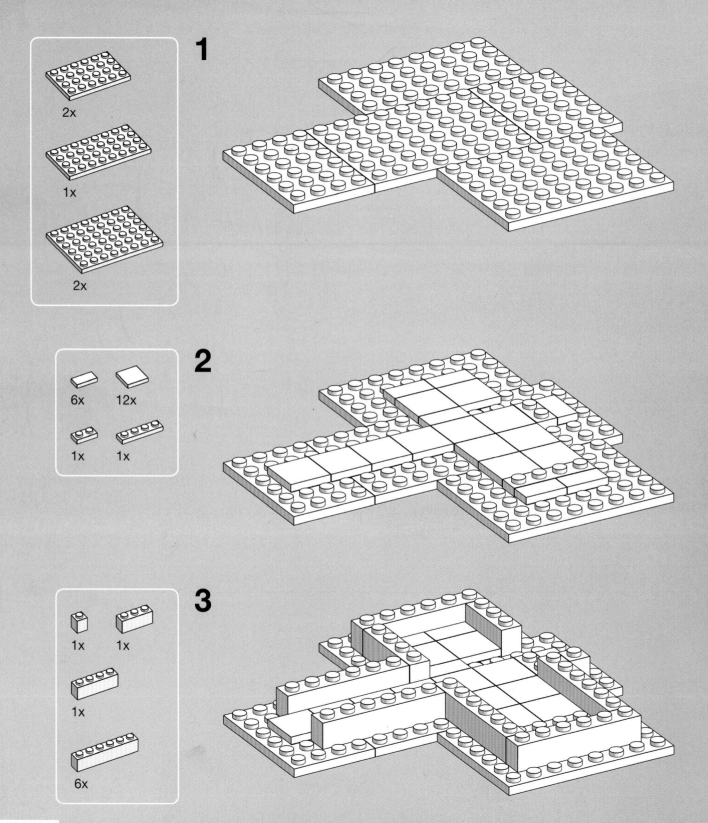

**1**

2x

1x

2x

**2**

6x  12x

1x  1x

**3**

1x  1x

1x

6x

**1**   **2**

6x

**1**   **2**

4x

**1**   **2**

1x

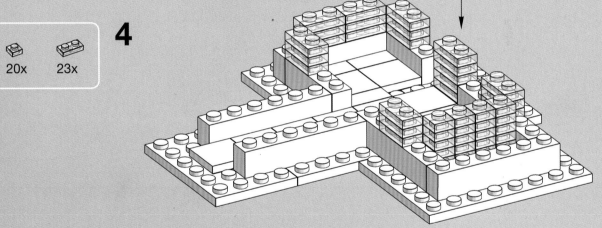

**4**

20x   23x

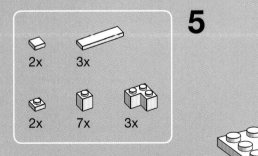

**5**

2x   3x

2x   7x   3x

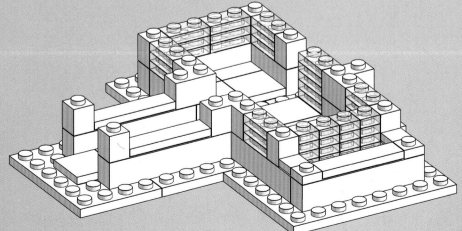

**1**  **2**  **3**  **4**

**6**

1x   1x

2x

3x

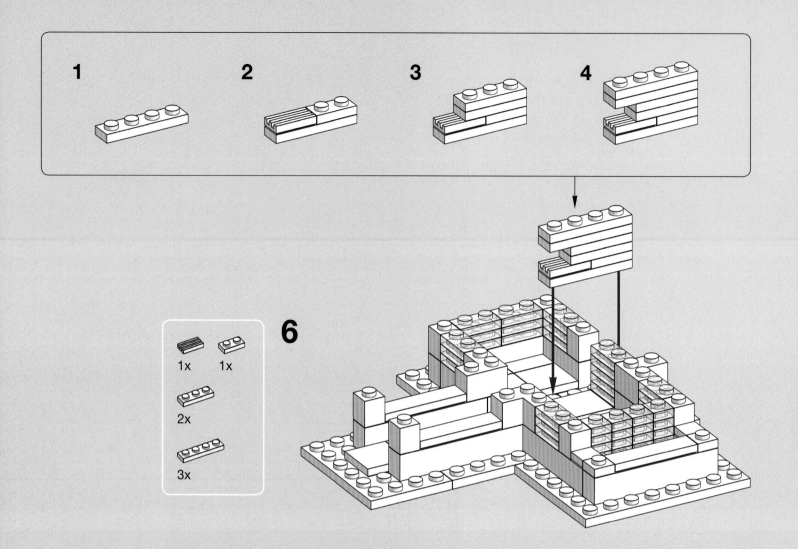

**7**

10x   1x   2x

2x   1x   2x

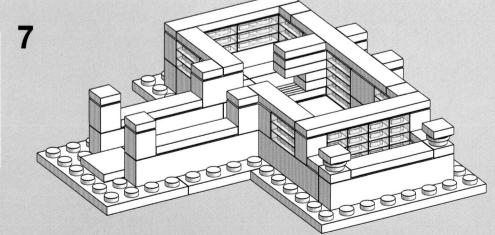

**8**

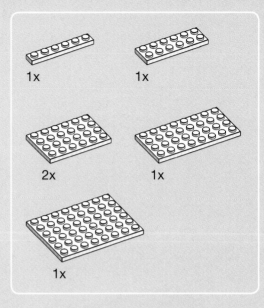

1x

1x

2x

1x

1x

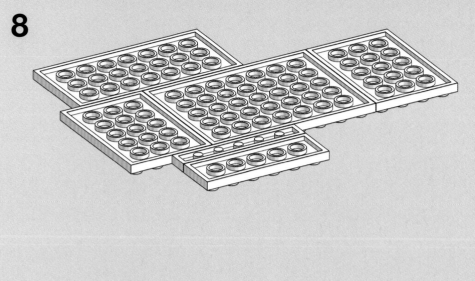

**9**

2x    2x

1x

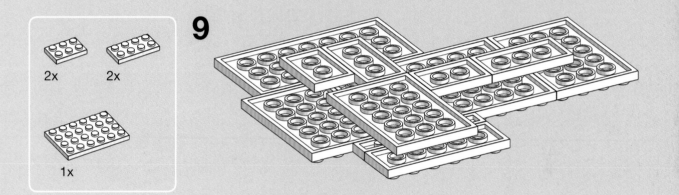

**10**

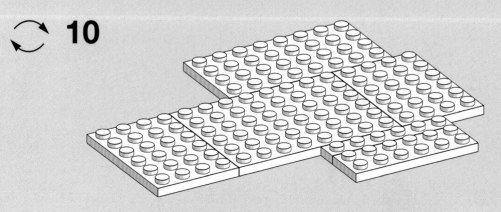

**11**

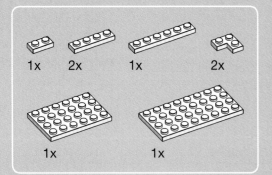

1x  2x  1x  2x

1x  1x

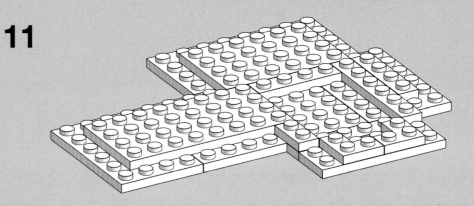

**12**

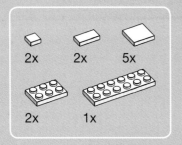

2x  2x  5x

2x  1x

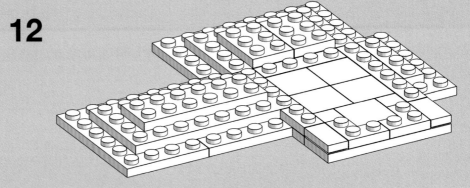

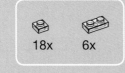

18x  6x

**1**  **2**

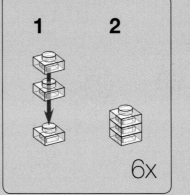

6x

**1**  **2**

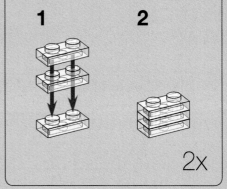

2x

**13**

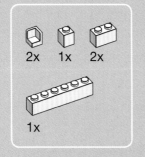

2x  1x  2x

1x

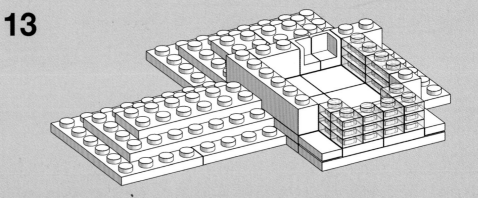

**14**

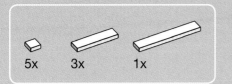

5x   3x   1x

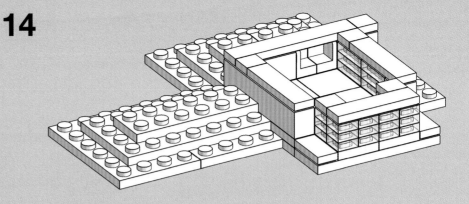

**15**

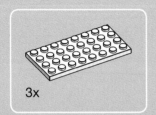

3x

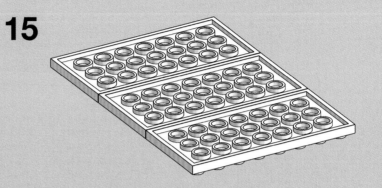

**16**

2x

1x

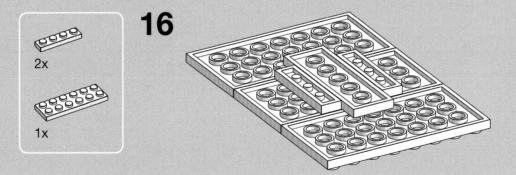

**17**

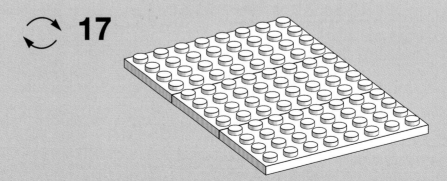

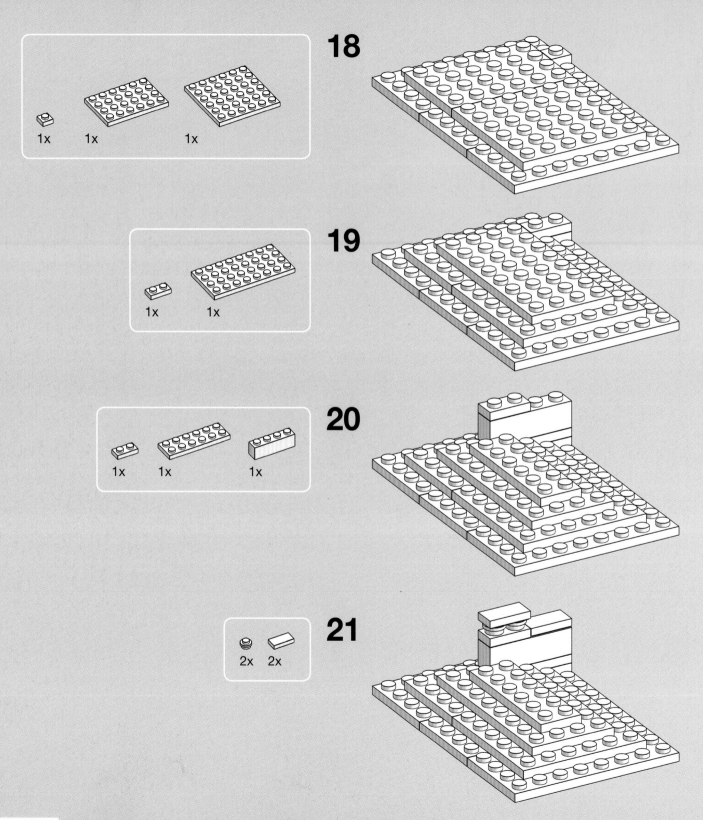

**18**

1x 1x 1x

**19**

1x 1x

**20**

1x 1x 1x

**21**

2x 2x

**22**

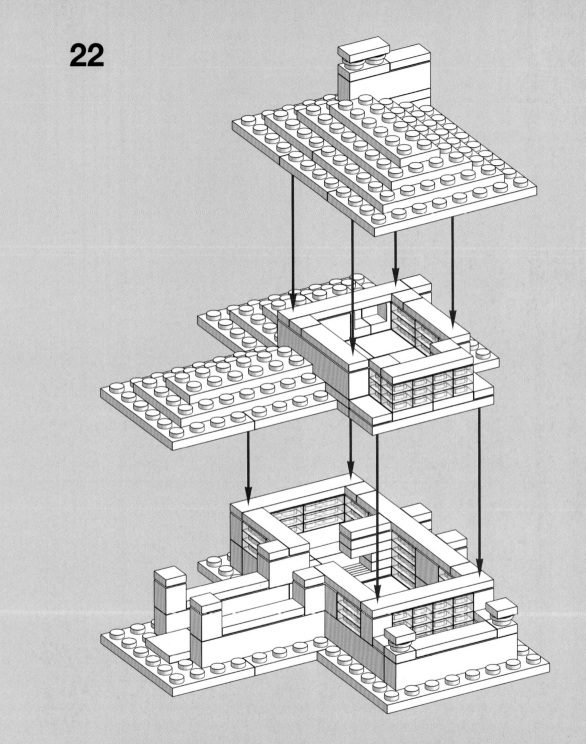

The lower floor shows how a continuous living space can be separated into different spaces by a fireplace (or hearth), small wall, or screen.

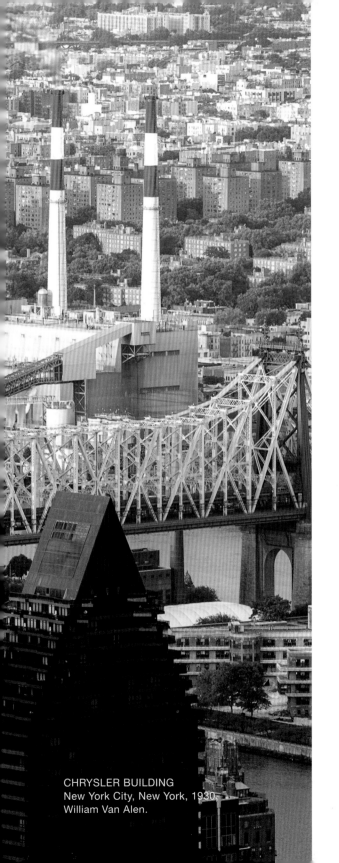

CHRYSLER BUILDING
New York City, New York, 1930.
William Van Alen.

# ART DECO

Art Deco is the exuberant architectural style born during the Roaring Twenties. Also known as the Jazz Age, this was a period of unprecedented wealth, fashion, and new technology. Buildings were clad in elaborate facades with intricate decorations to match the flamboyant times. The sky was the limit as developers raced to create the tallest skyscrapers.

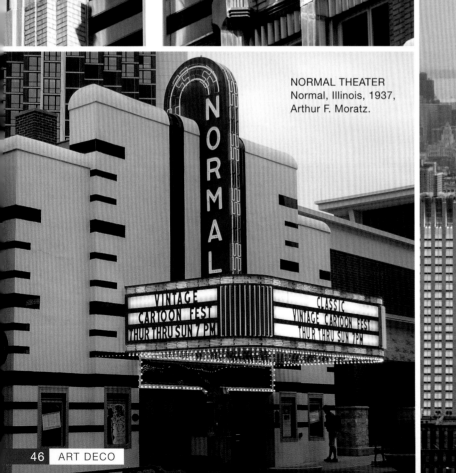

NIAGARA MOHAWK BUILDING
Syracuse, New York, 1932,
Bley & Lyman.

EMPIRE STATE BUILDING
New York City, New York, 1931,
Shreve, Lamb & Harmon.

NORMAL THEATER
Normal, Illinois, 1937,
Arthur F. Moratz.

The name *Art Deco* comes from the influential 1925 L'Exposition Internationale des Arts Décoratifs et Industriels Modernes in Paris, France. Many of the pavilions were built in this emerging architectural style. The artists who visited the exposition brought the Art Deco style to cities around the world, influencing all aspects of design, including furniture, clothing, jewelry, automobiles, and architecture.

Art Deco embraces the blocky abstractions of Cubism, with geometric designs that emphasize symmetry and repetition. The style borrows heavily from the Art Nouveau movement of 30 years prior, when architects re-created intricate organic forms using wood and iron. Many Art Deco designs were inspired by ancient Egyptian arts, sparked by the discovery of King Tutankhamun's tomb in 1922. As Art Deco grew into an international movement, architects drew inspiration from a range of other sources, including Native American, Mesoamerican, Japanese, and other historical motifs.

The wealth and unbridled enthusiasm of the 1920s fueled a race to build the world's tallest buildings. When a rival

## MATERIALS

Since Art Deco is rooted in applied ornamentation, architects explored a broad range of materials during the style's short history. Early buildings used high-end materials like copper, steel, and stone, while later examples used less-expensive materials like brightly colored stucco, tile, and glass blocks.

UNION TERMINAL
Cincinnati, Ohio, 1933,
Fellheimer & Wagner.

JERRY'S FAMOUS DELI
Miami Beach, Florida, 1940,
Henry Hohauser.

## LEGO BRICKS

Small slopes can be used to create the intricate patterns of early Art Deco.

Curved bricks are very useful when creating buildings in this style.

Tiles ensure that everything has a smooth, streamlined finish.

project threatened architect William Van Alen's plan to make the Chrysler Building the tallest building ever constructed, Van Alen built its now-iconic spire in secret. He mounted the 125-foot spire on top of the Chrysler Building in 1930, securing the record for the tallest building in the world. The honor didn't last long: 11 months later another Art Deco skyscraper, the more modestly decorated Empire State Building, would rise 400 feet higher.

Art Deco was popular in other buildings of this era, including offices, restaurants, and

apartments. Most common were movie theaters, which benefited from the tall, colorful, and brightly lit marquees. In many cases, the elaborate facades covered relatively simple, low-cost buildings.

As the Great Depression took hold in the 1930s, Art Deco evolved to use less costly materials like glass blocks and terra-cotta tiles. Heavily ornamented designs made way for Streamline Moderne, a new style based on aerodynamic forms that mimicked the shape of planes, trains, and automobiles. Some buildings were clad in reflective materials like glass and steel, as in the Daily Express Building (1936), which is curvy, simple, and unadorned. One of the last places where Art Deco remained popular was Miami Beach, Florida, where numerous hotels were built with bold symmetric designs, bright pastel hues, and neon lighting. This shift from ornate Art Deco buildings to simpler Streamline Moderne anticipated the next major shift in architecture, to International Style Modernism.

## ART DECO IN LEGO

As Art Deco is inherently decorative, you will want to spend time on the fine details. Specialty bricks and bright colors are an effective way to capture the energy and intricacy of the early Art Deco style. You'll need to find lots of curved parts if you want to capture the Streamline Moderne look. Many Art Deco buildings have intricate detailing on the building interior as well, so you may find this to be a fun style to explore when building larger, minifigure-scale models.

## LEGO COLORS

-  White
- Light bluish grey
- Medium blue
- Sand green
- Yellow
- Light pink
- Red
- Trans clear

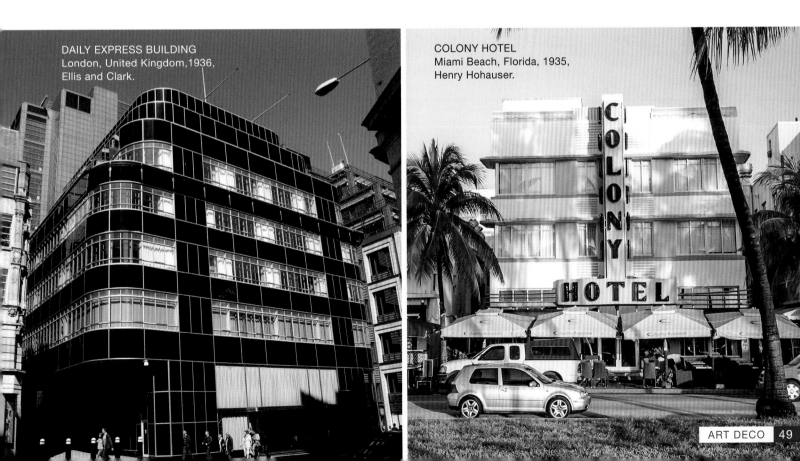

**DAILY EXPRESS BUILDING**
London, United Kingdom, 1936, Ellis and Clark.

**COLONY HOTEL**
Miami Beach, Florida, 1935, Henry Hohauser.

# ART DECO LEGO MODELS

OCEAN RESTAURAUNT
LEGO model by Andrew Tate.

COLONY HOTEL
Miami Beach, Florida, 1935, Henry Hohauser.
LEGO model by Daniel Siskind.

GALAXY DINER AND EMPIRE THEATER
LEGO model by Jonathan Grzywacz.

GUARDIAN BUILDING
Detroit, Michigan, 1929, Wirt C. Rowland.
LEGO model by Jim Garrett.

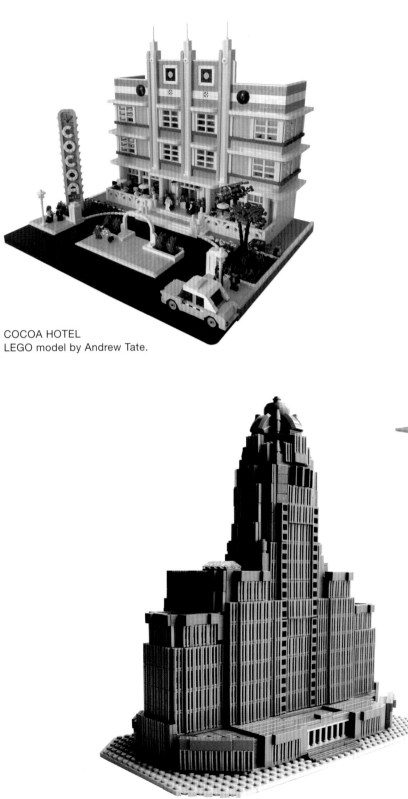

COCOA HOTEL
LEGO model by Andrew Tate.

MODULAR BANK
LEGO model by Dita Svelte.

BUFFALO CITY HALL
Buffalo, New York, 1931,
George J. Dietel and John J. Wade, with Sullivan W. Jones.
LEGO model by Thad Jantzi.

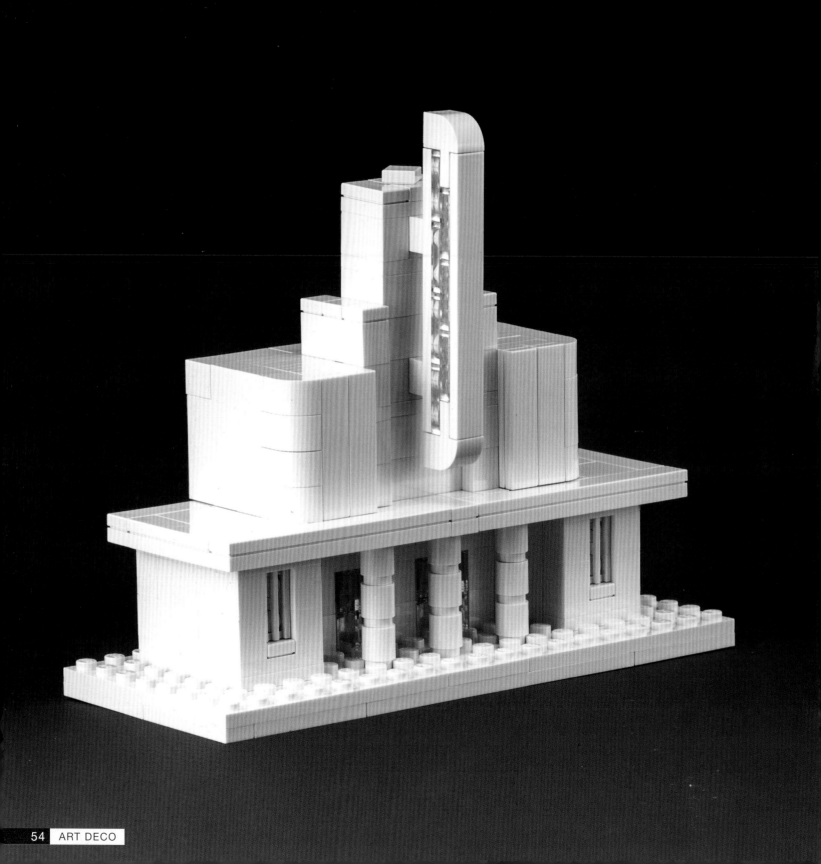

# MOVIE THEATER

This movie theater has a symmetrical facade with a prominent vertical marquee supported by stepped piers. It is inspired by the many great Art Deco theaters built in this period.

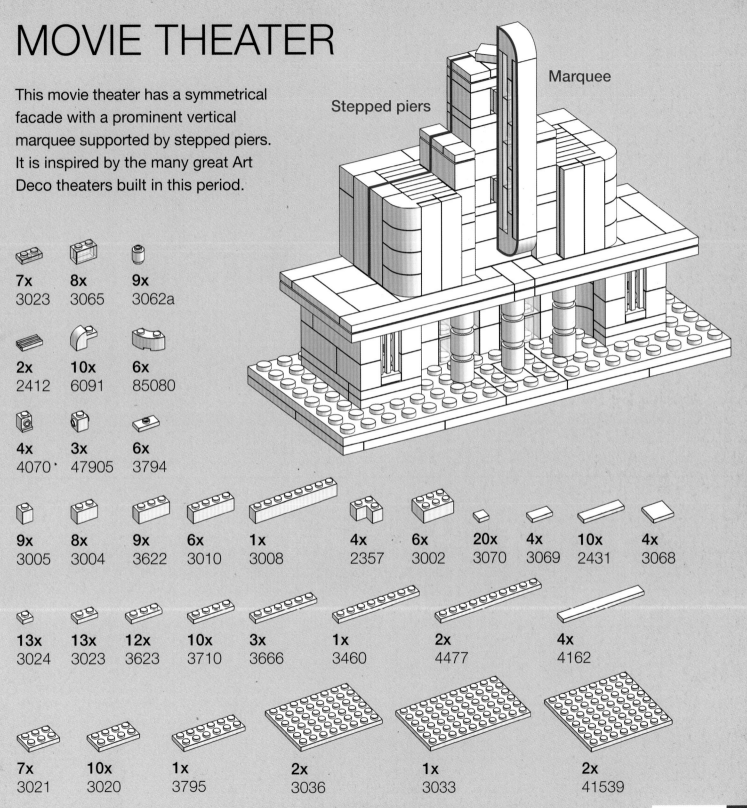

Stepped piers

Marquee

**7x**
3023

**8x**
3065

**9x**
3062a

**2x**
2412

**10x**
6091

**6x**
85080

**4x**
4070

**3x**
47905

**6x**
3794

**9x**
3005

**8x**
3004

**9x**
3622

**6x**
3010

**1x**
3008

**4x**
2357

**6x**
3002

**20x**
3070

**4x**
3069

**10x**
2431

**4x**
3068

**13x**
3024

**13x**
3023

**12x**
3623

**10x**
3710

**3x**
3666

**1x**
3460

**2x**
4477

**4x**
4162

**7x**
3021

**10x**
3020

**1x**
3795

**2x**
3036

**1x**
3033

**2x**
41539

**1**

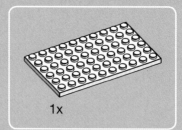

1x

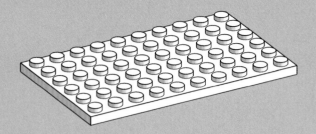

**2**

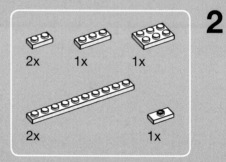

2x  1x  1x

2x  1x

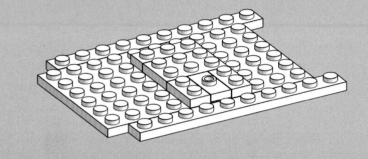

**3**

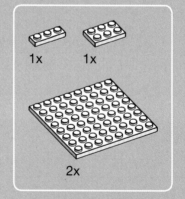

1x  1x

2x

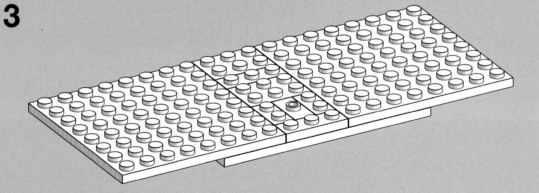

**4**

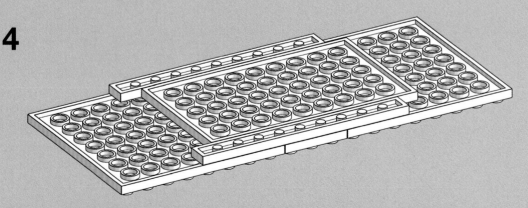

**5**

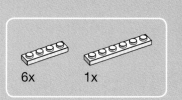

6x    1x

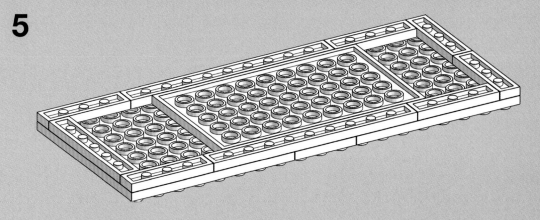

**6**

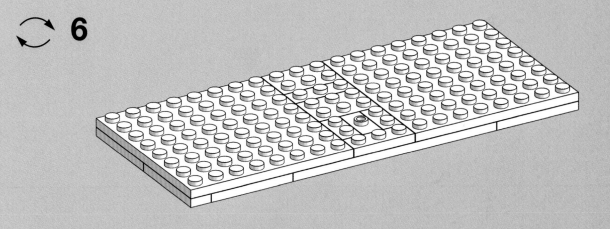

**7**

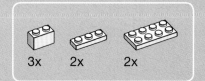

3x   2x   2x

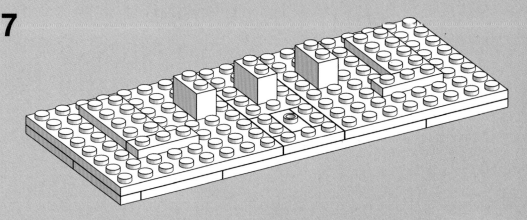

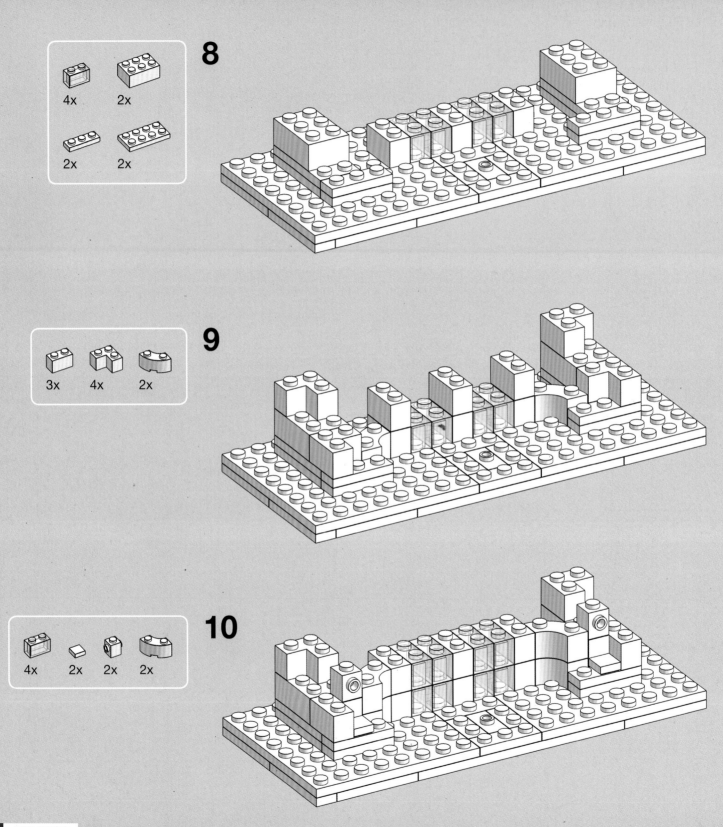

**8**

4x  2x
2x  2x

**9**

3x  4x  2x

**10**

4x  2x  2x  2x

**11**

2x  2x

**12**

3x  2x  2x

1x  1x

**13**

3x  2x

1x  1x

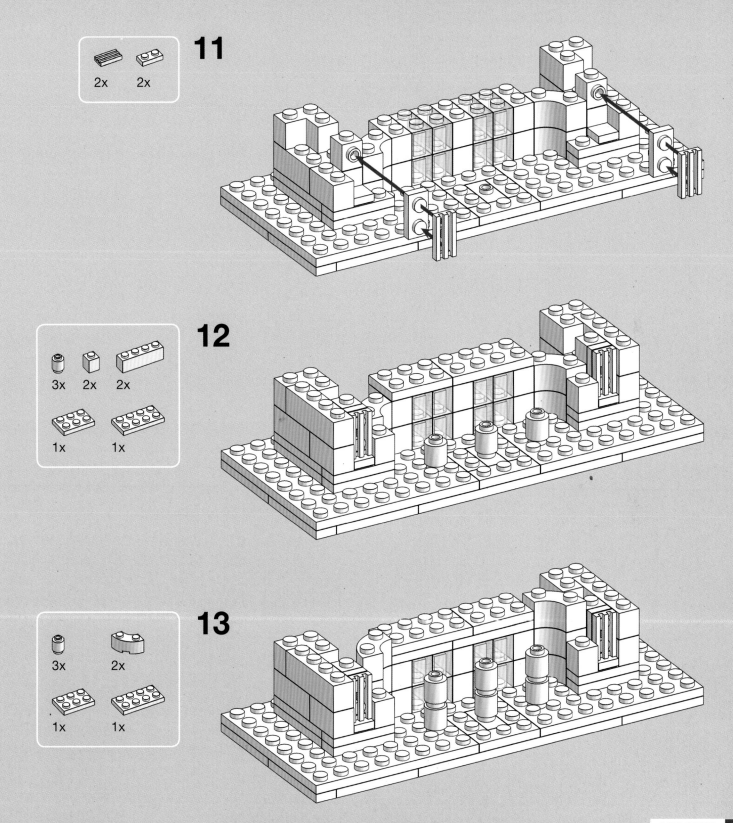

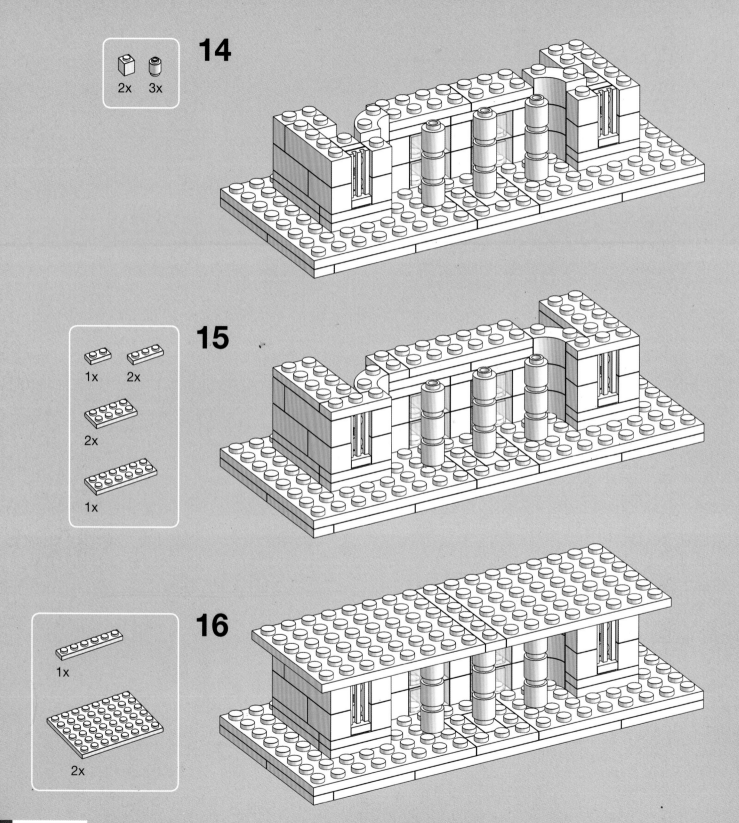

**14**

2x 3x

**15**

1x 2x

2x

1x

**16**

1x

2x

**17**

3x 2x

4x

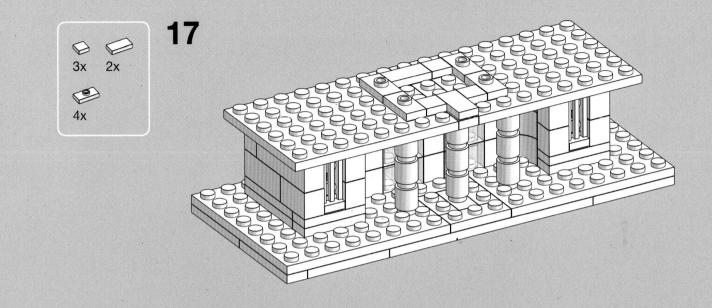

**18**

1x 6x

3x

4x

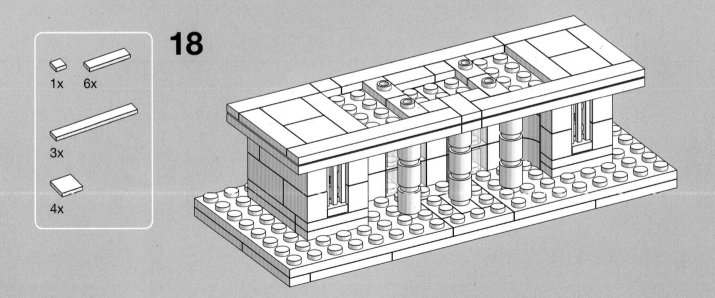

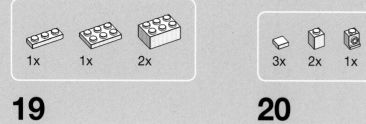

**19**

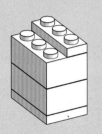

**20**

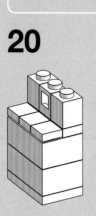

**21**

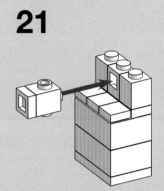

**22**

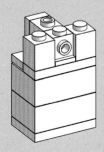

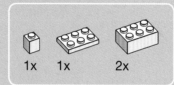

**23**

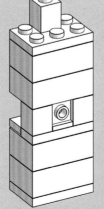

**24**

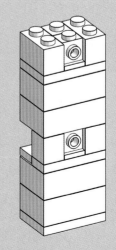

**28**

3x  1x

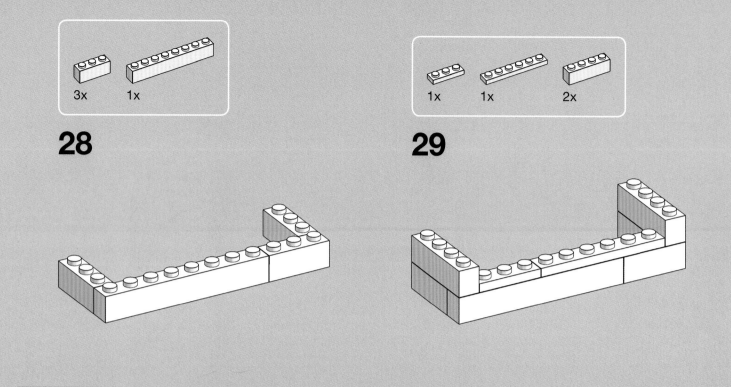

**29**

1x  1x  2x

**30**

2x  2x  2x

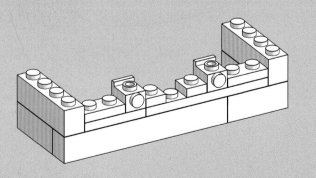

**31**

2x  2x  2x

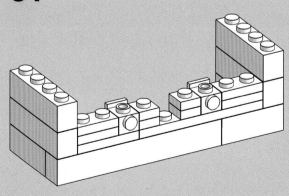

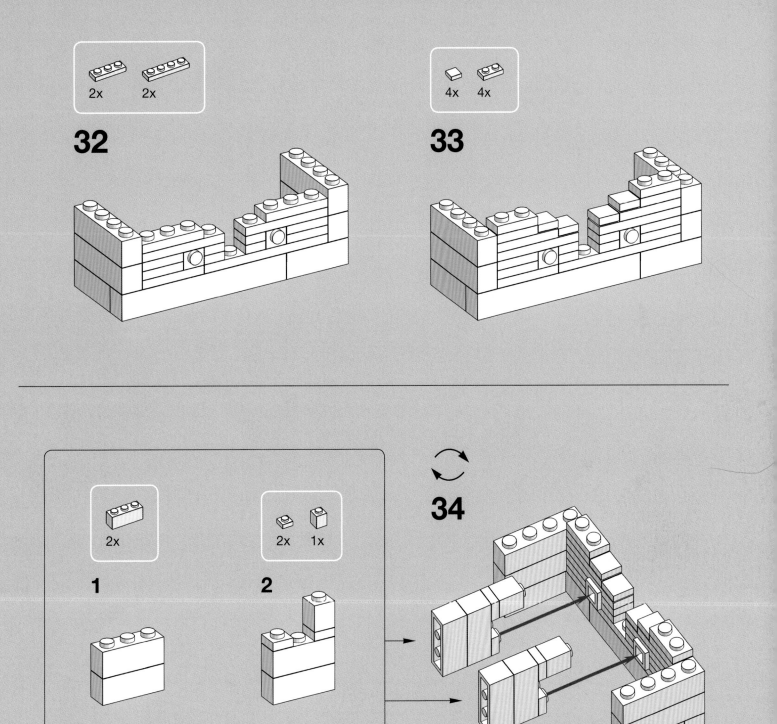

**32**

2x  2x

**33**

4x  4x

**1**

2x

**2**

2x  1x

2x

**34**

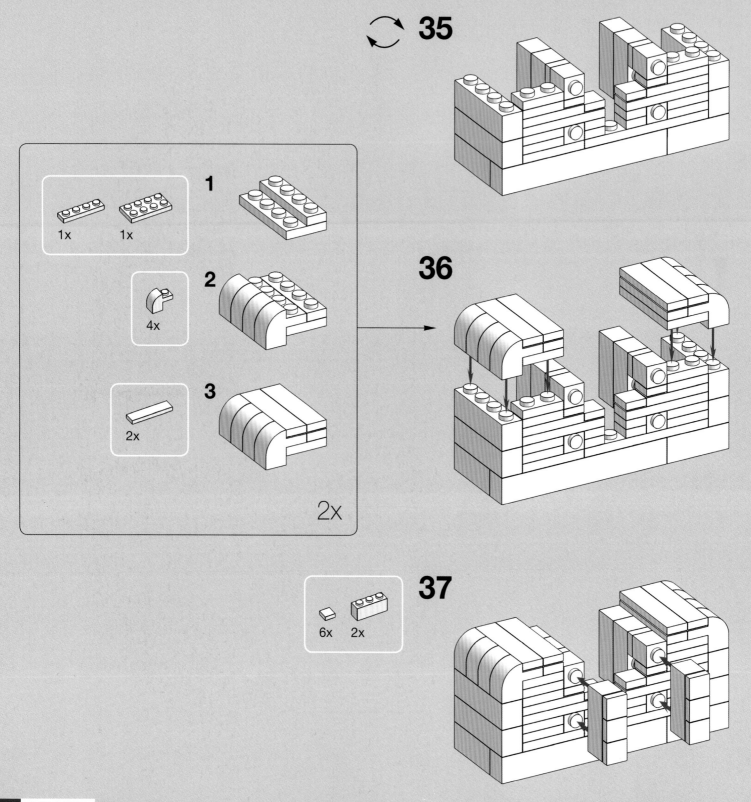

# 38

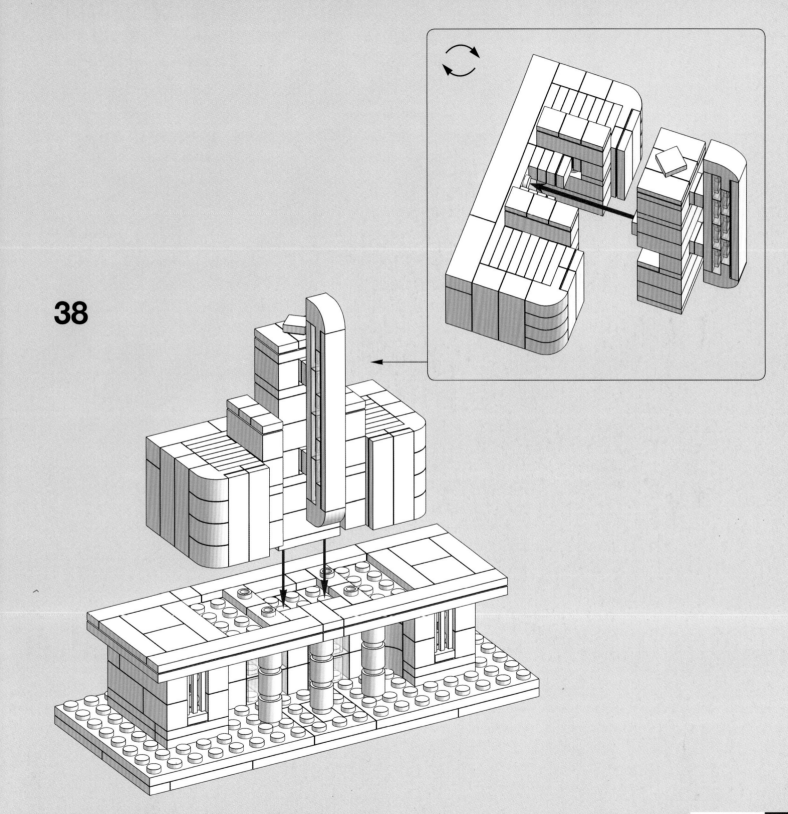

FARNSWORTH HOUSE
Plano, Illinois, 1951,
Mies van der Rohe.

# MODERNISM

"Less is more."
—Mies van der Rohe

## CURTAIN WALL

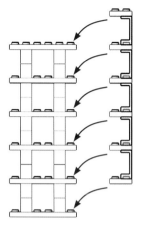

The curtain wall hangs from the central support structure of the building.

Modernism sprang from the convergence of new industrial materials and a new philosophy of building where "form follows function," a phrase coined in 1896 by architect Louis Sullivan. Sullivan is often considered the first Modernist architect because he was one of the first to embrace steel framing in the construction of tall buildings, instead of using load-bearing masonry walls. This cut costs and gave buildings more usable interior space as it allowed for much thinner walls. These early skyscrapers have the same skeleton as modern-day glass towers but were clad with a masonry exterior to match other buildings of their era.

The earliest buildings to feature a truly Modernist exterior came out of the Bauhaus, a school in Germany that taught modern industrial design, arts, and architecture. In 1926, the school moved into the Bauhaus Dessau, a large new building designed by founder Walter Gropius. The building was one of the first to have floor-to-ceiling curtain-wall windows that hung from a steel frame instead of being supported from below.

By 1932, there were enough buildings in this emerging style that an international exhibition of architecture was organized at the newly established Museum of Modern

WAINWRIGHT BUILDING
St. Louis, Missouri, 1891,
Adler & Sullivan.

LAKE SHORE DRIVE
Chicago, Illinois, 1951,
Mies van der Rohe.

BAUHAUS DESSAU
Dessau, Germany, 1926,
Walter Gropius.

Art in New York City. *Modern Architecture— International Exhibition* was so successful that it gave this early phase of Modernism its own name: the International Style. The show featured buildings that followed the three Modernist principles: emphasis of volume over mass, regularity and standardization of elements, and avoidance of ornamentation.

Emphasizing volume over mass creates brightly lit buildings, such as Mies van der Rohe's Barcelona Pavilion (1929), where the indoor and outdoor spaces are separated only by glass walls. Regularity and standardization of elements are clearly present in Le Corbusier's Villa Savoye (1931), through the use of identical concrete columns (or *pilotis*) that support the second story. Lovell Health House (1929) by Richard Neutra is an example of a building with an interesting form but minimal ornamentation.

Soon after the 1929 exhibition, the Bauhaus dissolved as Germany slipped into the hands of the Nazi Party, driving many architects to find new homes around the world. Meanwhile in the United States, Frank Lloyd Wright, famous for his Prairie-style

Glass, metal, and concrete are the most common materials in Modernist architecture. In the 1950s, concrete was generally used only for structural elements of Modernist buildings, but by the 1960s, architects were leaving concrete visible in finished buildings, a trend that eventually evolved into a new style, Brutalism.

MILLER HOUSE
Palm Springs, California, 1937,
Richard Neutra.

WILLIS TOWER
Chicago, Illinois, 1973,
Skidmore, Owings & Merrill.

EAMES HOUSE
Los Angeles, California, 1949,
Charles and Ray Eames.

homes, was reborn as a Modernist architect with Fallingwater in 1937. In placing a modern yet cozy home atop a waterfall, Wright created one of the most famous homes ever built.

The International Style wouldn't find mainstream appeal until after World War II when its growth was fueled by economic prosperity, especially in the United States. Mies van der Rohe pushed the limits of the Modernist philosophy of architecture with Farnsworth House (1951). By reducing the human needs of a vacation home to their logical extreme, the house is little more

than a glass box that vanishes into the landscape.

Advocates of Modernist architecture hoped to create a new template for modern living to meet the growing demand for housing in the postwar period. The Case Study House project in Los Angeles, sponsored by *Arts & Architecture* magazine, challenged leading Modernist architects to design small single-family homes that would be inexpensive to construct. More than 30 homes were designed and published in the magazine, including Eames House (1949), a colorful loft home built of

BARCELONA PAVILION
Barcelona, Spain, 1929,
Mies van der Rohe.

prefabricated industrial materials. Despite these efforts, Modernist homes weren't appealing to many families.

In contrast, office buildings like Lever House (1952) showed that you could build attractive cubic skyscrapers if you clad them in glass. Modernist architecture became the dominate corporate style for the next 35 years as businesses learned that buildings with large open floor plans were more profitable to rent and cheaper to construct than more decorated styles.

The basic rectangular skyscraper was copied all over the world with varying results.

By the late 1960s, architects started looking for ways to inject some of their own style while preserving the efficiency of Modernist designs. The stair-stepped Sears Tower (1973), now called Willis Tower, added visual interest by staggering the building's height as it rises. Oscar Niemeyer added sculptural shapes to Modernist buildings, as in the curved shapes he used instead of basic columns

FALLINGWATER
Mill Run, Pennsylvania, 1937,
Frank Lloyd Wright.

PALÁCIO DO PLANALTO
Brasilia, Brazil, 1960,
Oscar Niemeyer.

for Palácio do Planalto (1960). By the 1980s, new buildings had become more and more decorated, ushering in the Postmodern era.

## MODERNISM IN LEGO

Modernism is a natural fit for LEGO as the style rarely deviates from blocky, cubic forms, especially those buildings in the early International Style. That said, building large sections of glass can be difficult because there is a limited number of clear LEGO parts.

Because of Modernism's lack of orna-mentation, you might find it challenging to build interesting models. Focusing on the principle of emphasizing volume over mass can be helpful: try making interesting shapes using only basic LEGO bricks to represent whole rooms or floors. Once you have a basic form that you like, you can re-create it with windows, pilotis, and other details. If it doesn't look quite right, change the proportions by making the model taller or wider, or incorporate a simple repeated element such as horizontal or vertical bands of a different color.

You can also try placing your model in a landscape. A model with simple lines and colors can be really striking when placed on a hill or surrounded with greenery.

### LEGO COLORS

- White
- Light bluish grey
- Black
- Trans light blue
- Trans clear

# MODERNIST
# LEGO MODELS

VILLA AMANZI
Phuket, Thailand, 2008, Original Vision Ltd.
LEGO model by Robert Turner.

VILLA HILLCREST
LEGO model by Ken, Amethel,
and Kai Parel-Sewell.

MODERN HOME
LEGO model by Dave Kaleta.

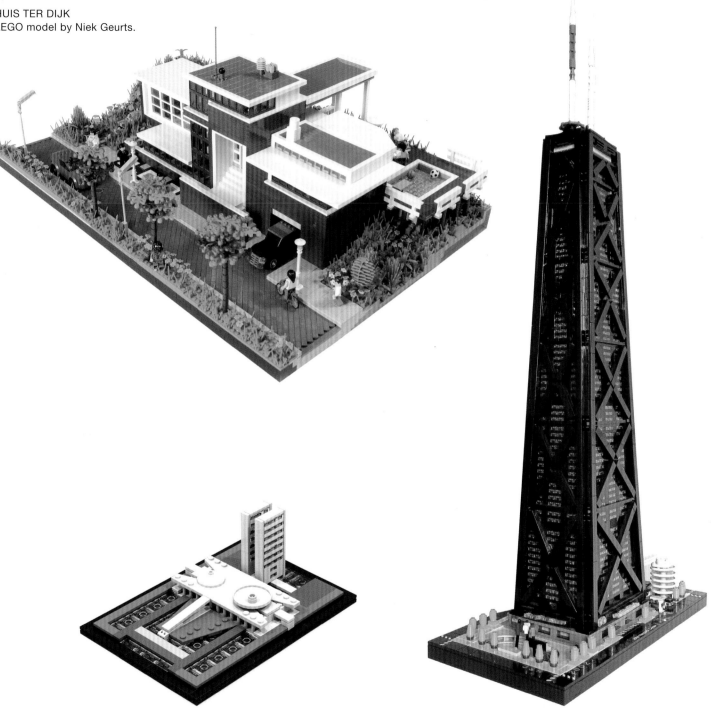

HUIS TER DIJK
LEGO model by Niek Geurts.

NATIONAL CONGRESS OF BRAZIL
Brasília, Brazil, 1964, Oscar Niemeyer.
LEGO model by Paul Wellington.

JOHN HANCOCK CENTER
Chicago, Illinois, 1969, Skidmore, Owings & Merrill.
LEGO model by Spencer Rezkalla.

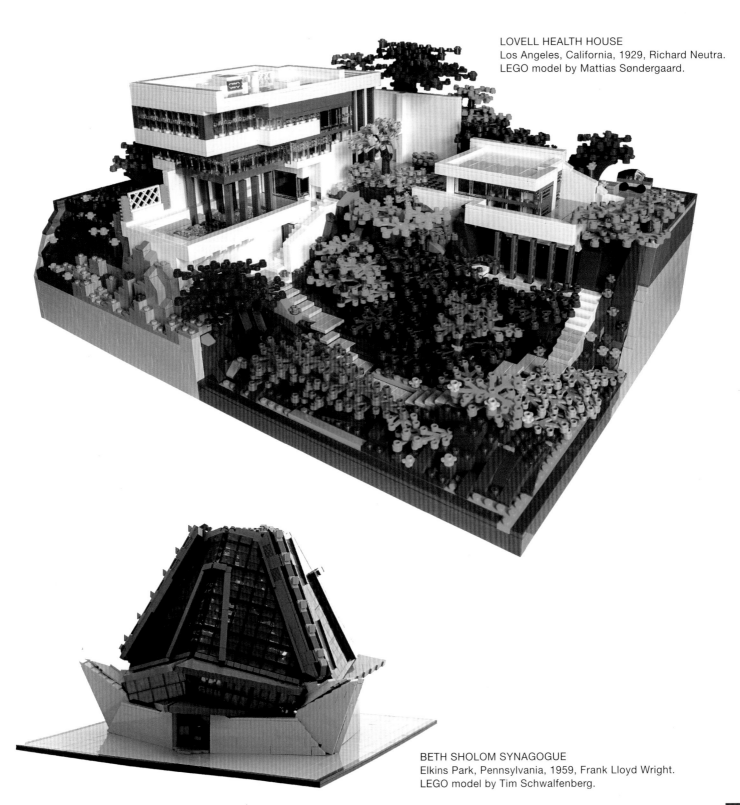

LOVELL HEALTH HOUSE
Los Angeles, California, 1929, Richard Neutra.
LEGO model by Mattias Søndergaard.

BETH SHOLOM SYNAGOGUE
Elkins Park, Pennsylvania, 1959, Frank Lloyd Wright.
LEGO model by Tim Schwalfenberg.

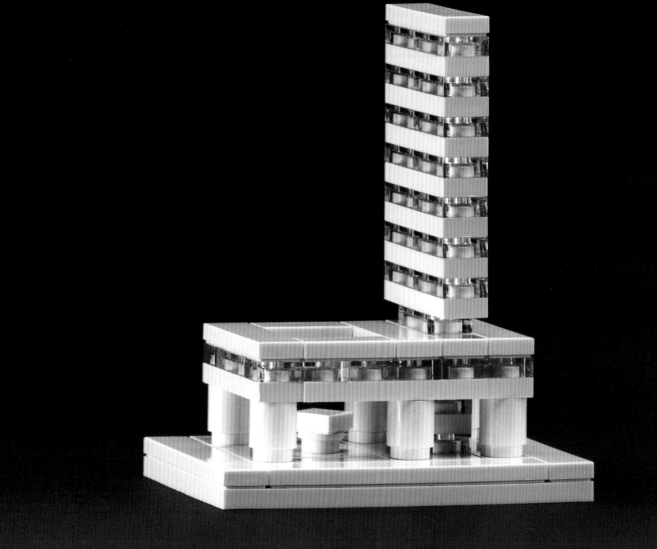

# LEVER HOUSE

Lever House is an International Style office tower in New York City. It is one of the earliest office buildings in this style and has been designated as a landmark. It features a broad second story that surrounds a public courtyard, and a single slender tower.

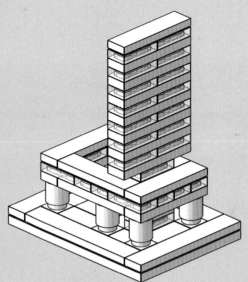

LEVER HOUSE
New York City, New York, 1952,
Skidmore, Owings & Merrill.

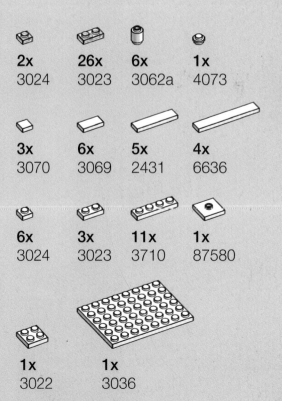

| 2x | 26x | 6x | 1x |
|---|---|---|---|
| 3024 | 3023 | 3062a | 4073 |

| 3x | 6x | 5x | 4x |
|---|---|---|---|
| 3070 | 3069 | 2431 | 6636 |

| 6x | 3x | 11x | 1x |
|---|---|---|---|
| 3024 | 3023 | 3710 | 87580 |

| 1x | 1x |
|---|---|
| 3022 | 3036 |

**1**

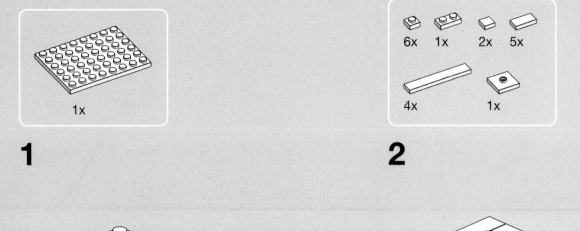

1x

**2**

6x 1x 2x 5x

4x 1x

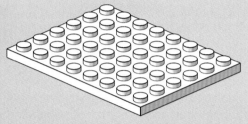

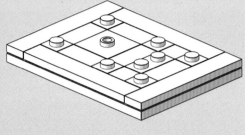

**3**

2x 1x 1x 1x

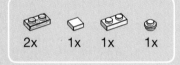

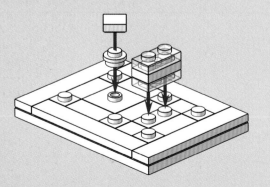

**4**

6x

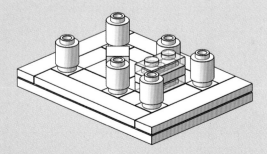

**1** 4x 1x

**2** 2x 9x

**3** 1x 4x 1x

**5**

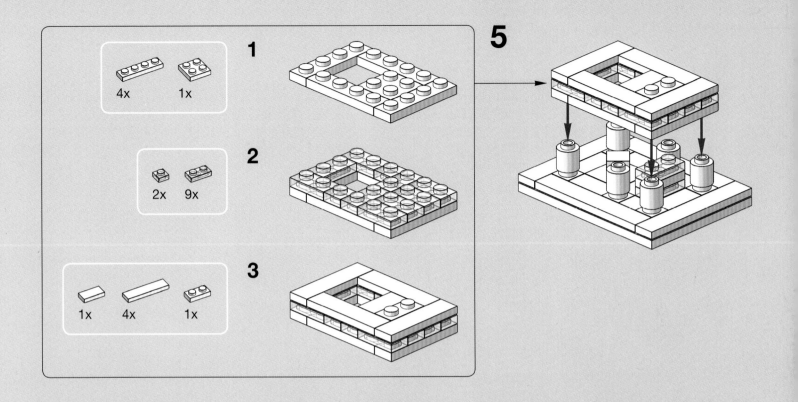

**6**

15x 1x 7x

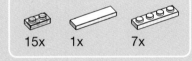

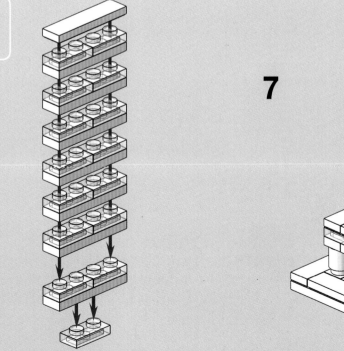

**7**

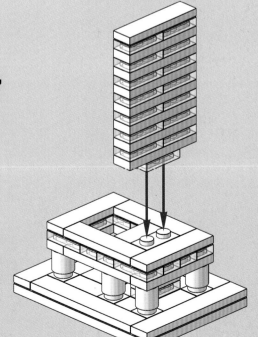

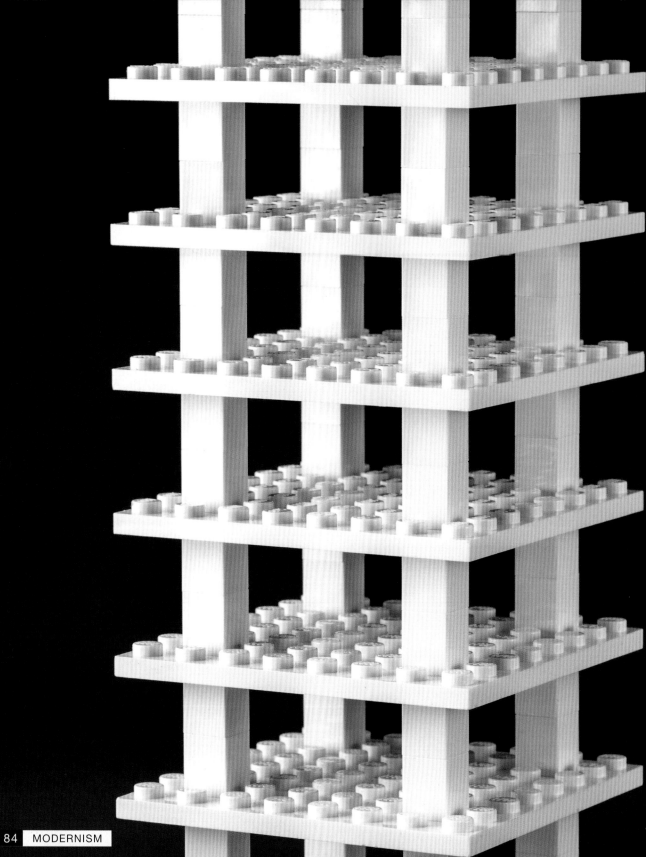

# LOAD-BEARING STRUCTURE

Most Modernist skyscrapers are built around a load-bearing structure, often built with steel and concrete. The building's exterior looks solid, but in reality, it hangs from the central structure like a curtain. A glass and aluminum exterior is most common, but more-traditional materials like stone, brick, or wood are sometimes used. We'll use this load-bearing structure as the base for the next two models.

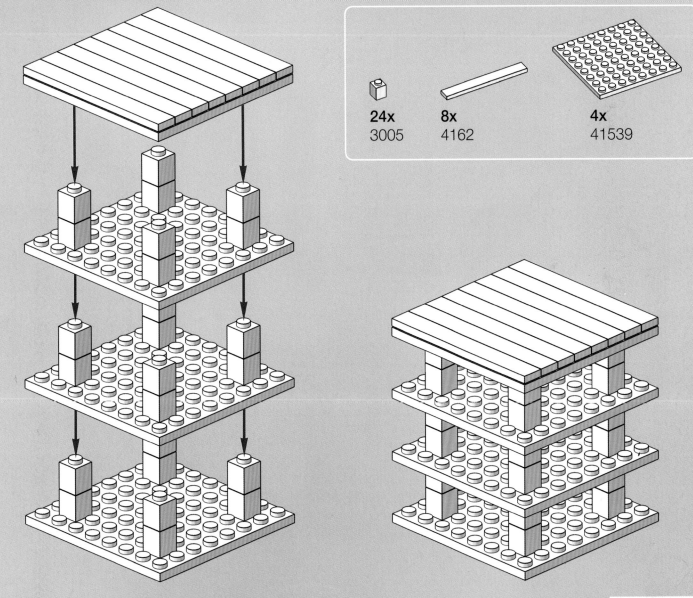

| 24x | 8x | 4x |
|-----|-----|-----|
| 3005 | 4162 | 41539 |

# CURTAIN-WALL BUILDING

This is a simple Modernist curtain-wall exterior that you can hang from the basic load-bearing structure on page 85. You can modify this design to create a larger or smaller building.

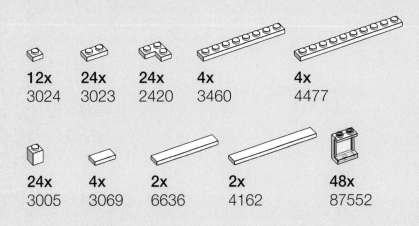

**12x**
3024

**24x**
3023

**24x**
2420

**4x**
3460

**4x**
4477

**24x**
3005

**4x**
3069

**2x**
6636

**2x**
4162

**48x**
87552

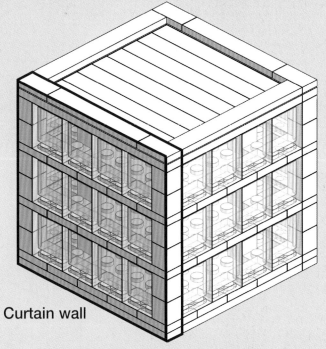

Curtain wall

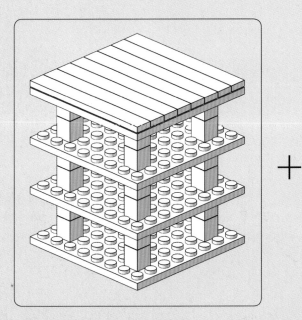 +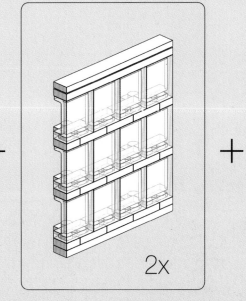

2x

+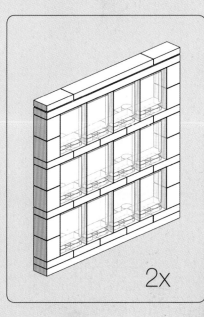

2x

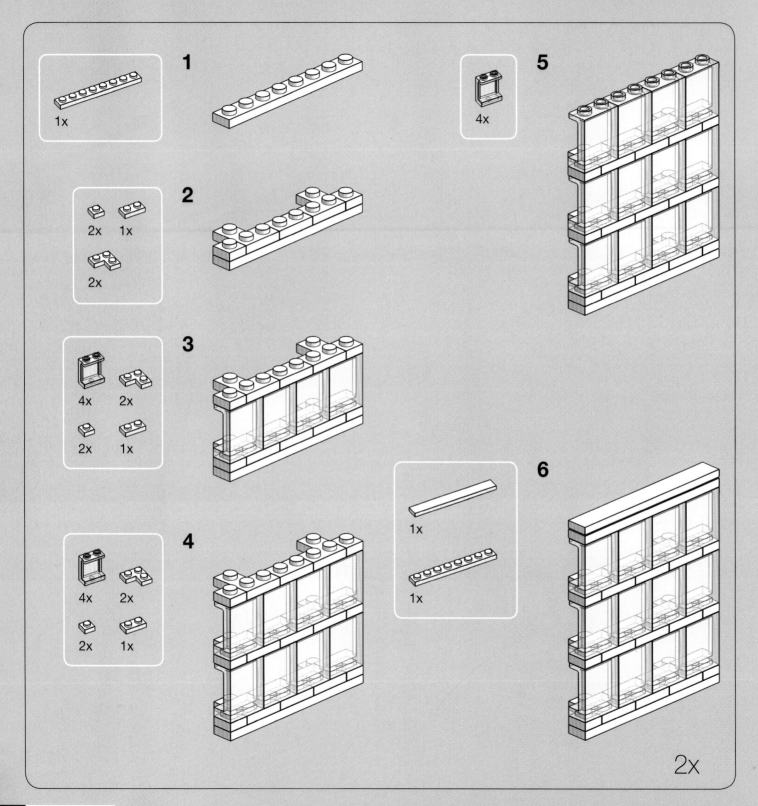

**1**

**2**

**3**

**4**

**5**

**6**

1x

2x 1x

2x

4x 2x

2x 1x

4x 2x

2x 1x

4x

1x

1x

2x

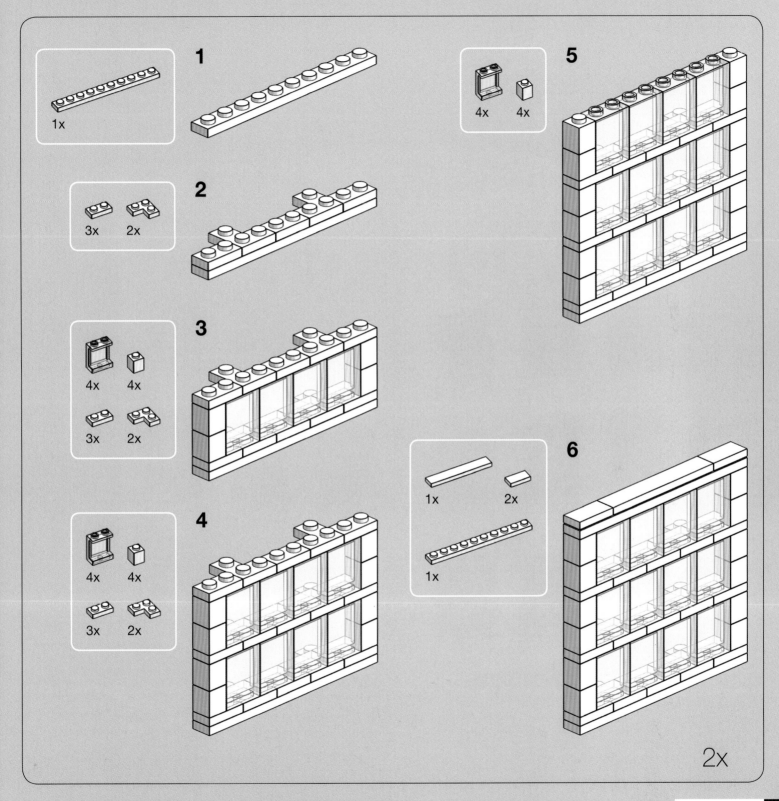

# SULLIVANESQUE BUILDING

This exterior is in the style of early skyscrapers by Louis Sullivan, but this model uses the same load-bearing structure (from page 85) as the curtain-wall building.

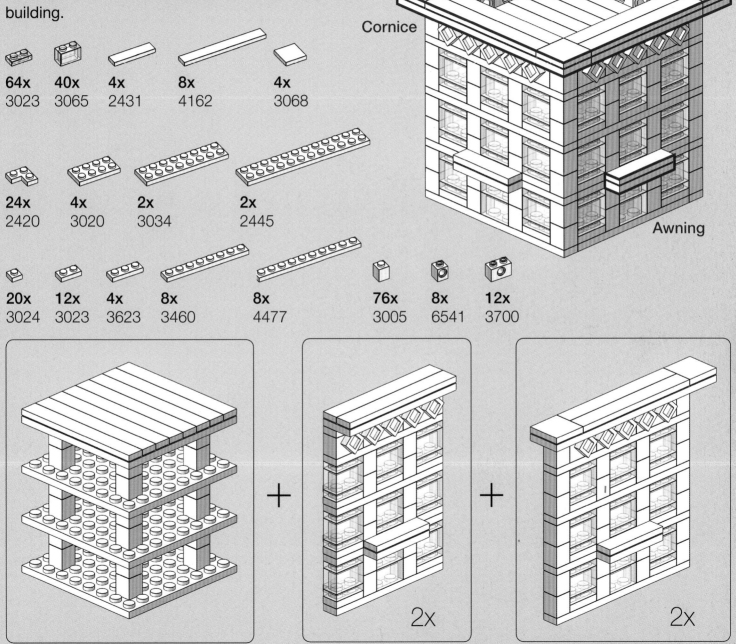

**64x** 3023  **40x** 3065  **4x** 2431  **8x** 4162  **4x** 3068

**24x** 2420  **4x** 3020  **2x** 3034  **2x** 2445

**20x** 3024  **12x** 3023  **4x** 3623  **8x** 3460  **8x** 4477  **76x** 3005  **8x** 6541  **12x** 3700

Cornice

Awning

+  2x  +  2x

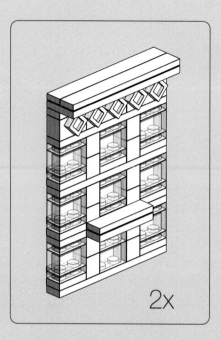

2x

**1**

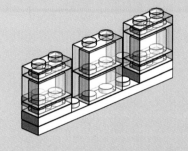

**2**

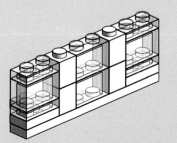

**3**

**4**

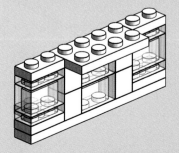

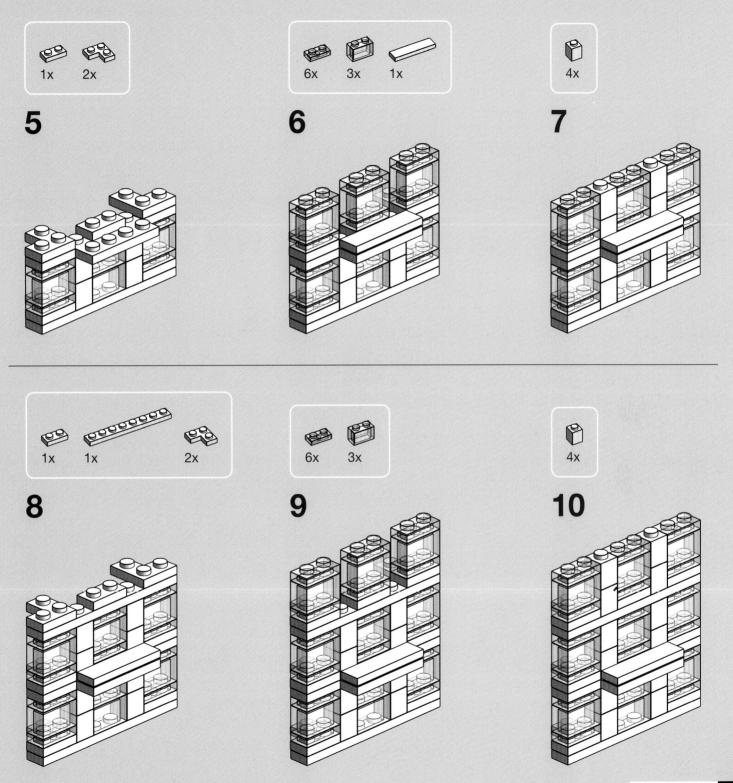

**5**

**6**

**7**

**8**

**9**

**10**

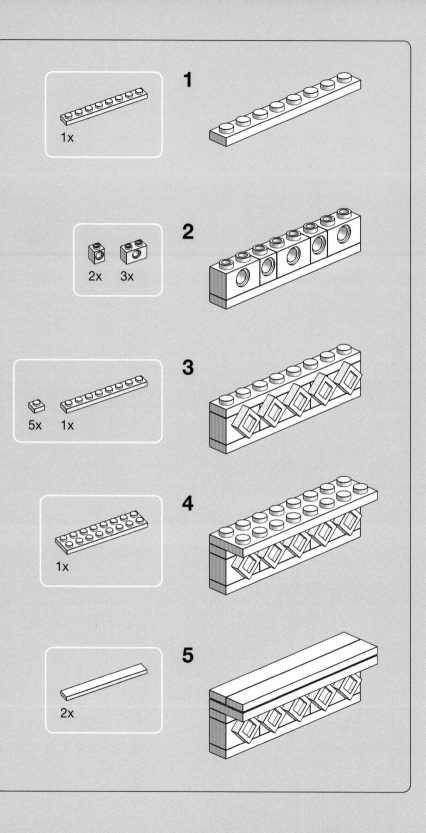

**11**

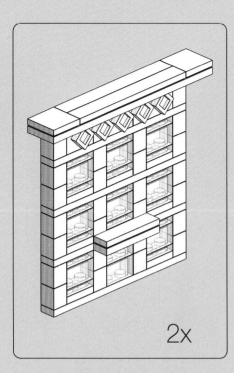

2x

**1**

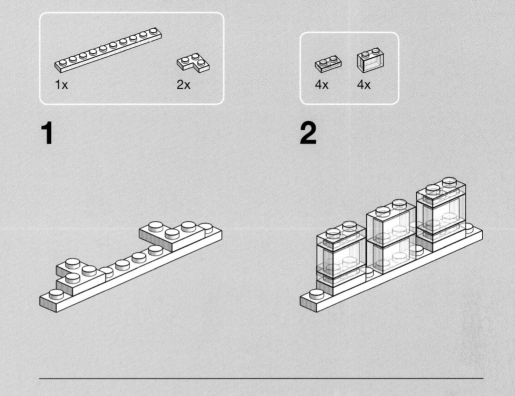

1x 2x

**2**

4x 4x

**3**

8x

**4**

2x 1x

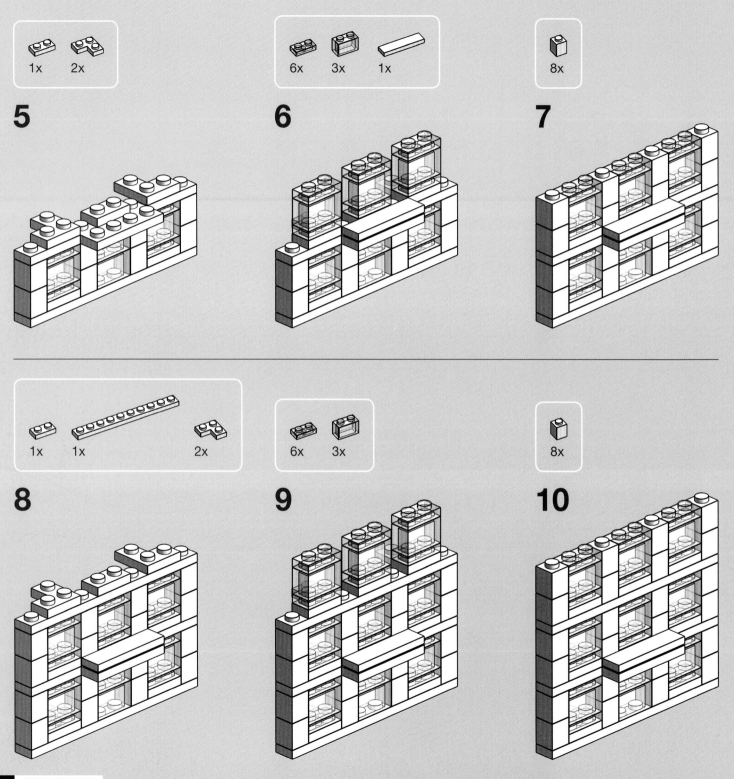

**11**

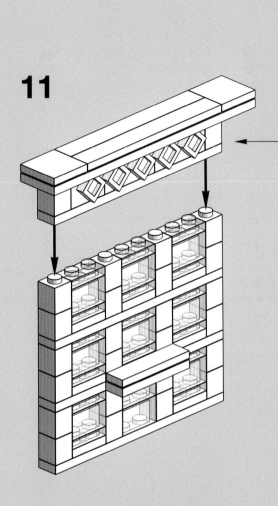

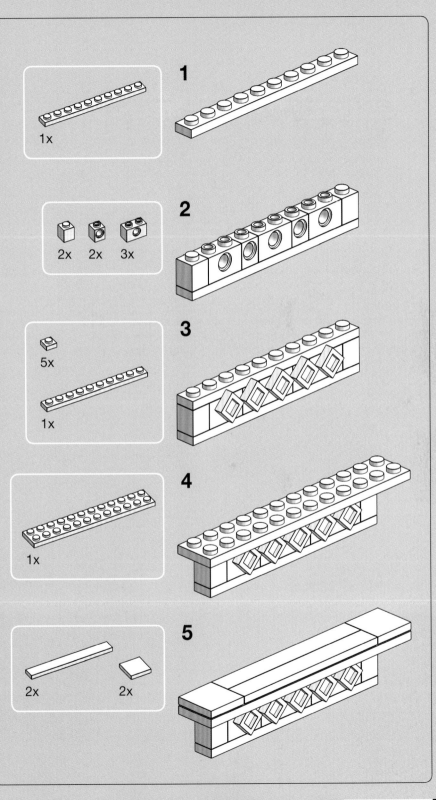

**1**

1x

**2**

2x  2x  3x

**3**

5x

1x

**4**

1x

**5**

2x  2x

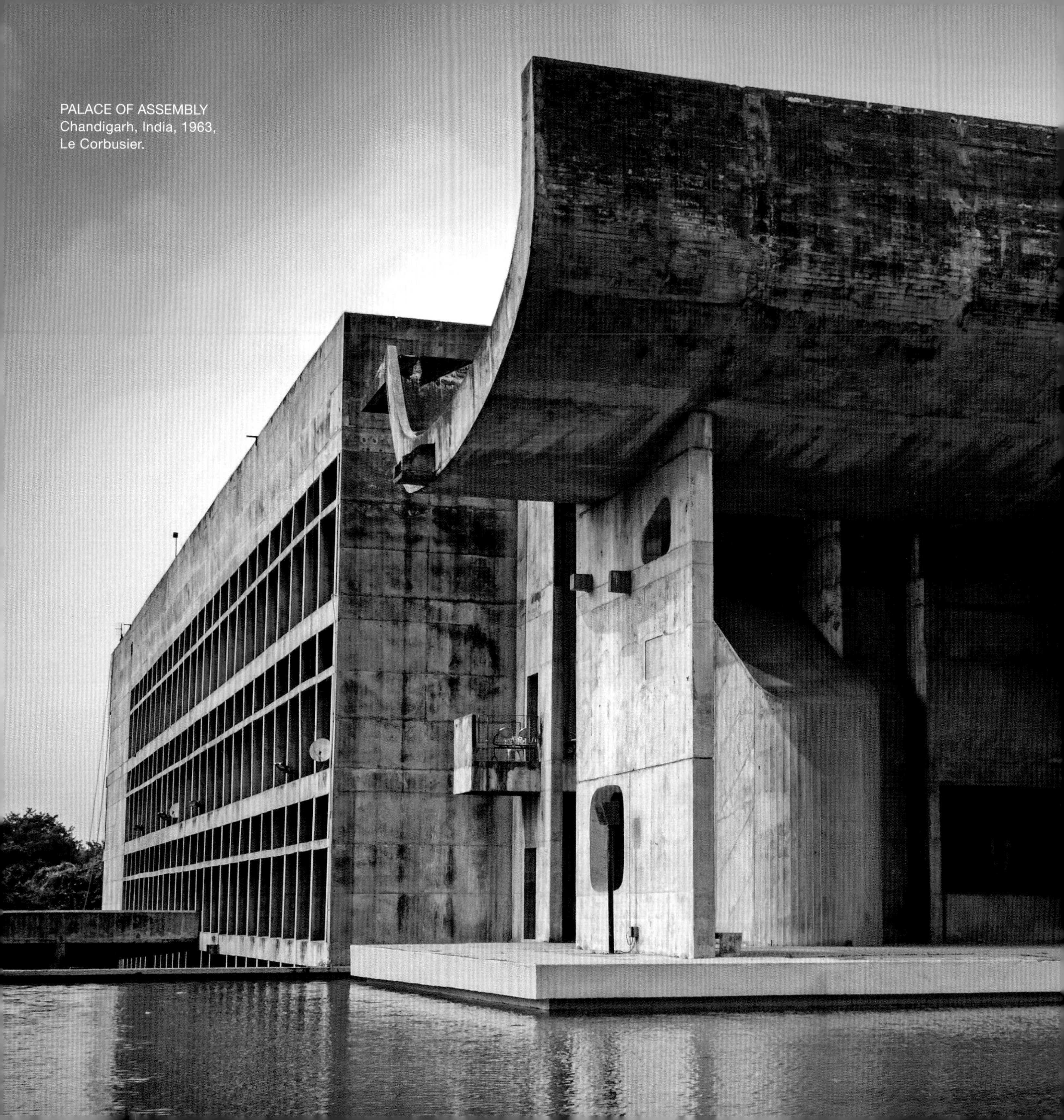

PALACE OF ASSEMBLY
Chandigarh, India, 1963,
Le Corbusier.

# BRUTALISM

Brutalism is an offshoot of Modernism that exploits the creative potential of reinforced concrete. Because concrete is usually poured on site, architects are free to explore new and unfamiliar shapes, limited only by their ability to create a temporary form to support the concrete as it cures. Concrete is a low-cost building material, which has made Brutalism a popular style for cost-sensitive public projects such as universities, government buildings, and public housing.

UNITÉ D'HABITATION OF BERLIN
Berlin, Germany, 1957,
Le Corbusier.

Many people assume that the name *Brutalism* comes from the architecture's angular, aggressive, and raw look, which could easily be described as "brutal." However, it is actually derived from the term *béton brut* (or "raw concrete"), which the architect Le Corbusier used in many of his buildings. Le Corbusier is probably most famous for Villa Savoye (1931), which is generally credited as a Modernist design, but his later Unité d'Habitation (1952) is a monument of concrete and a clear example of the early Brutalist style.

The versatility of raw concrete has allowed architects to create a wide variety of sculptural forms. Brutalist buildings can be sharply angular as in Andrew Melville Hall (1967), employ blocky cubic forms like Habitat 67 (1967), feature smooth curves, or combine all of the above, such as with Palace of Assembly (1963) in Chandigarh, India. Many buildings follow strict symmetry, while others have more unpredictable forms. Small, oddly shaped windows are common—a frequent criticism of the style by the people who live and work in these buildings.

Although Brutalism was a leading style throughout the late 1960s and early 1970s, a subsequent period of strongly negative

### LEGO CONCRETE TEXTURES

The grooves in these bricks mimic the textures left behind when concrete forms are removed.

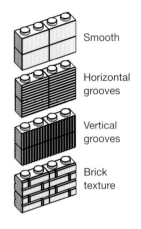

Smooth

Horizontal grooves

Vertical grooves

Brick texture

**ANDREW MELVILLE HALL**
St Andrews, Scotland, 1967,
James Stirling.

**SALK INSTITUTE**
La Jolla, California, 1962,
Louis Kahn.

ROBARTS LIBRARY
University of Toronto, Canada, 1973,
Mathers & Haldenby.

GOVERNMENT SERVICE CENTER
Boston, Massachusetts, 1971,
Paul Rudolph.

### LEGO BRICKS

 Regular bricks can create large blocky forms quickly.

 Slopes add interesting angles to your model.

 Inverted slopes let your building get wider as it gets taller.

 Round bricks can create contrast with sharp angles.

attitudes led to the destruction of many Brutalist buildings. The negativity is understandable: many Brutalist buildings were cheaply made to meet the immediate needs of growing cities for subsidized housing and other services.

Fortunately, a new generation of architects and architecture enthusiasts is pushing past these preconceived notions. Many of the finest Brutalist buildings that remain standing have been protected as landmarks, and a Neobrutalist style has emerged in recent years. These new designs tend to focus on the sculptural

capabilities of concrete and the ability to create structures on a massive scale, rather than on mere cost savings. This is evident in the Phæno Science Center (2005), which blends Brutalist construction techniques with an abstract, Deconstructivist form.

### BRUTALISM IN LEGO

Many Brutalist buildings have rectangular forms that are easy to re-create using LEGO bricks. Architect Moshe Safdie even used LEGO bricks to help design Habitat 67, as he explained in a 2014 interview: "I bought all the LEGO

HABITAT 67
Montreal, Canada, 1967,
Moshe Safdie.

in Montreal at the time because we built many alternatives. The 2×1 brick was perfect for the cluster studies."

A growing selection of LEGO bricks makes it possible to create a model with angles and curves, but you may find it difficult to re-create a specific building because of limited shapes. If you want to build Brutalist buildings with complex forms, you may prefer to create buildings of your own design. For inspiration, try combining curved and angled bricks in many different ways.

**LEGO COLORS**

White

Light bluish grey

Dark bluish grey

Tan

Trans clear

PHÆNO SCIENCE CENTER
Wolfsburg, Germany, 2005,
Zaha Hadid.

UNITÉ D'HABITATION
Marseille, France, 1952, Le Corbusier.
LEGO model designed by Ken Parel-Sewell and built by Dan Madryga.

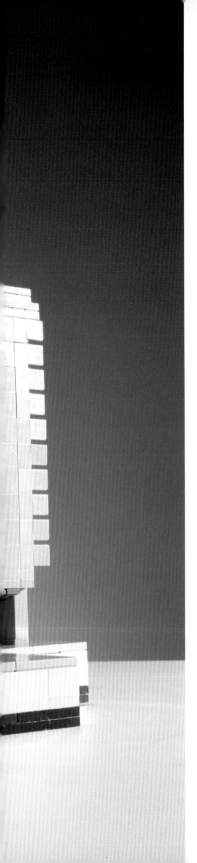

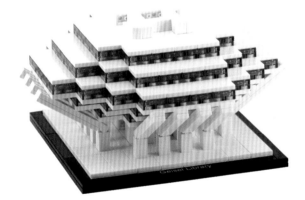

UNIVERSITY OF WATERLOO,
MATHEMATICS & COMPUTER BUILDING
Waterloo, Canada, 1968. LEGO model by Jason Allemann.

GEISEL LIBRARY
San Diego, California, 1970,
Pereira & Associates.
LEGO model by Tom Alphin.

HABITAT 67
Montreal, Canada, 1967, Moshe Safdie.
LEGO model by Nathalie Boucher.

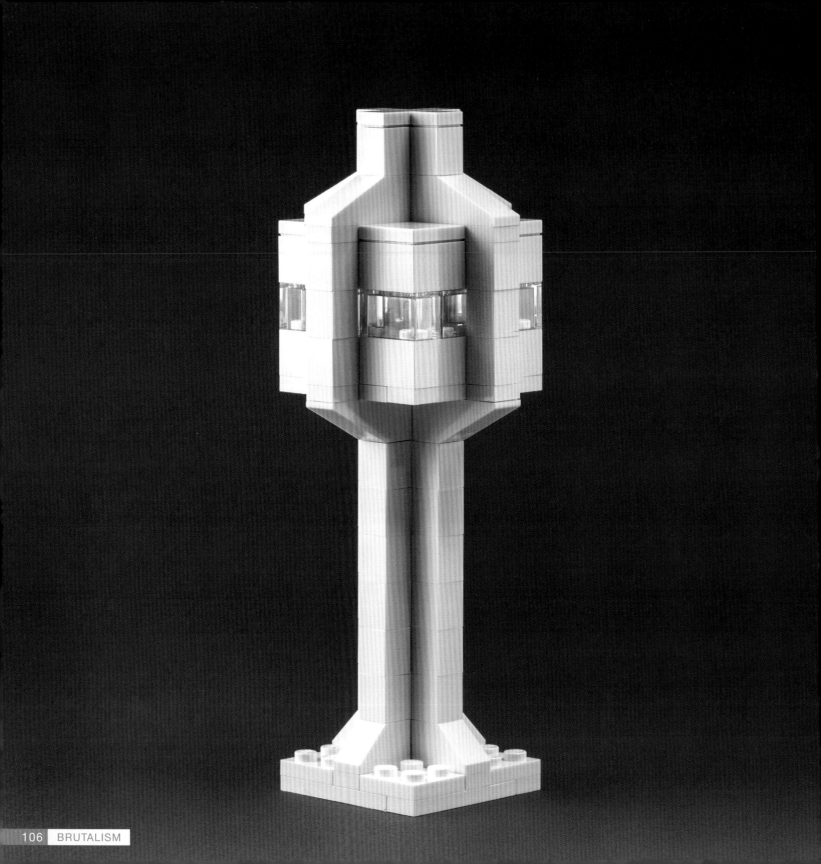

# AIR TRAFFIC CONTROL TOWER

This tower features the angular construction typical of
many Brutalist designs, although it is not based on a
specific building. Many air traffic control towers at large
international airports have a similar stalk-like design,
built out of reinforced concrete. While it is possible for
architects to create curved shapes using concrete,
a blocky design with sharp angles is more common
because it is cheaper to construct.

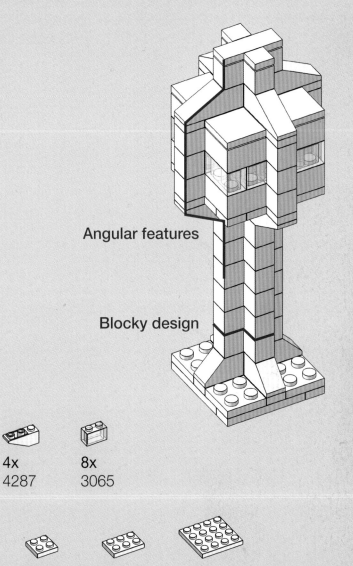

Angular features

Blocky design

| 21x | 6x | 10x | 4x | 4x |
|---|---|---|---|---|
| 3005 | 3004 | 3622 | 2357 | 3003 |

| 2x | 1x | 4x | 4x | 4x | 4x | 8x |
|---|---|---|---|---|---|---|
| 3070 | 63864 | 3068 | 3040 | 4286 | 4287 | 3065 |

| 6x | 3x | 4x | 6x | 1x | 4x | 1x | 1x |
|---|---|---|---|---|---|---|---|
| 3024 | 3023 | 3623 | 3710 | 3666 | 3022 | 3021 | 3031 |

**1**

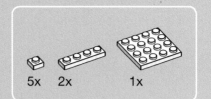

5x 2x 1x

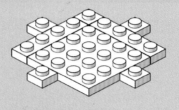

**2**

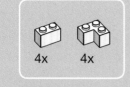

4x 4x

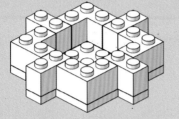

**3**

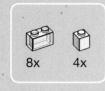

8x 4x

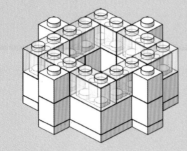

**4**

4x 4x

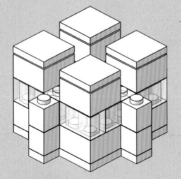

**5**

2x 3x

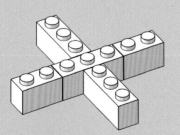

**6**

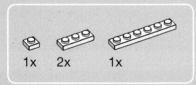

1x 2x 1x

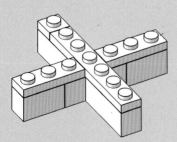

**7**

**8**

**9**

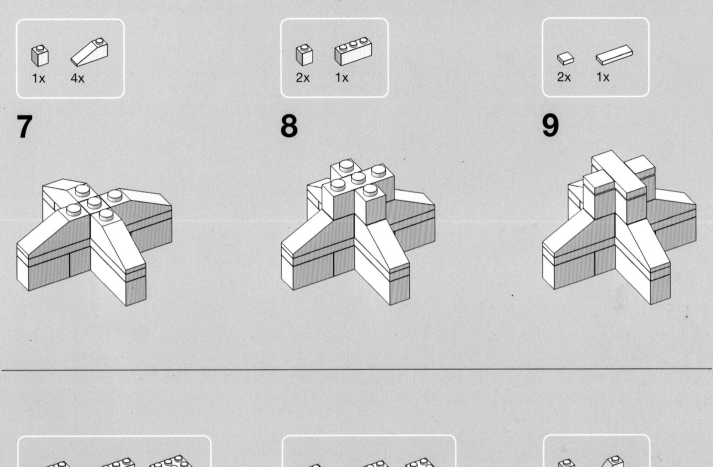

**10**

**11**

**12**

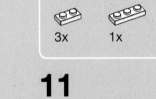

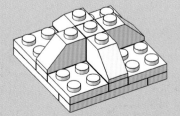

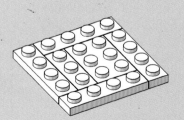

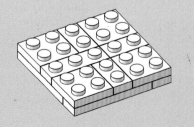

**13**

12x 6x

**14**

1x 4x

**15**

**16**

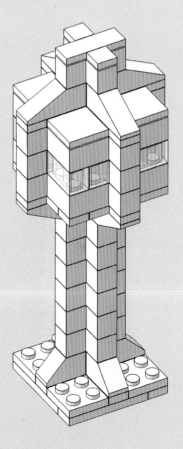

AIR TRAFFIC CONTROL TOWER
Tampa International Airport,
Tampa, Florida.

# GLASS LIBRARY

This building has a bold, rational, and unquestionably Brutalist form despite the large windows, which are uncommon for the style. This model is loosely based on the Geisel Library (1970) in San Diego, California. The angular concrete supports allow for cantilevered upper floors that are wider than the base of the building.

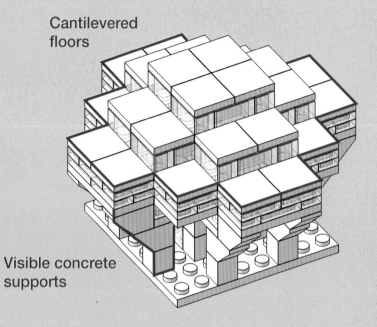

Cantilevered floors

Visible concrete supports

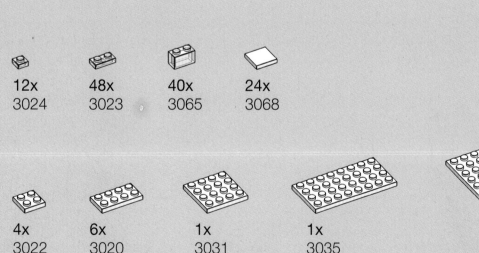

12x
3005

4x
3622

16x
3665

12x
3024

48x
3023

40x
3065

24x
3068

4x
3022

6x
3020

1x
3031

1x
3035

1x
41539

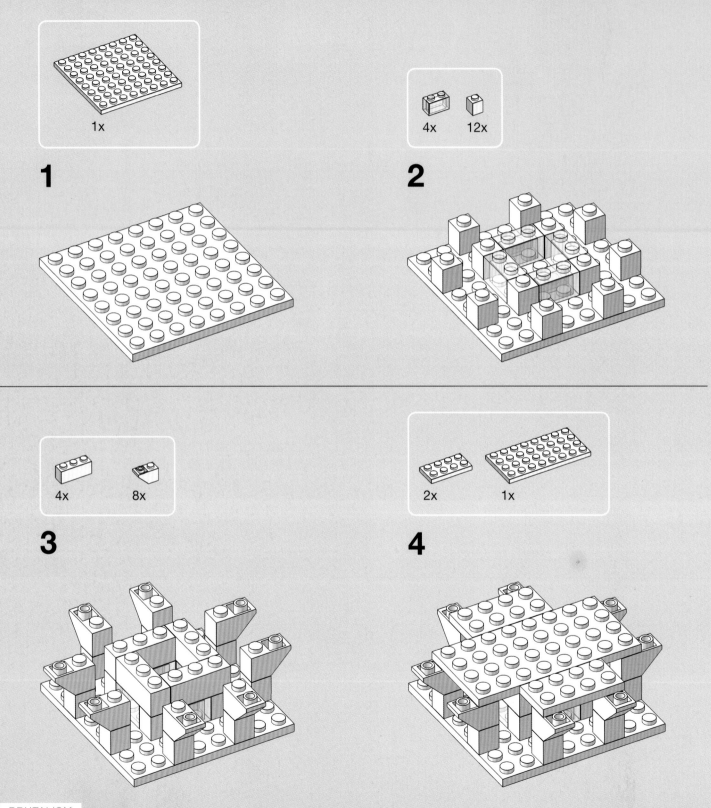

**1**

1x

**2**

4x 12x

**3**

4x 8x

**4**

2x 1x

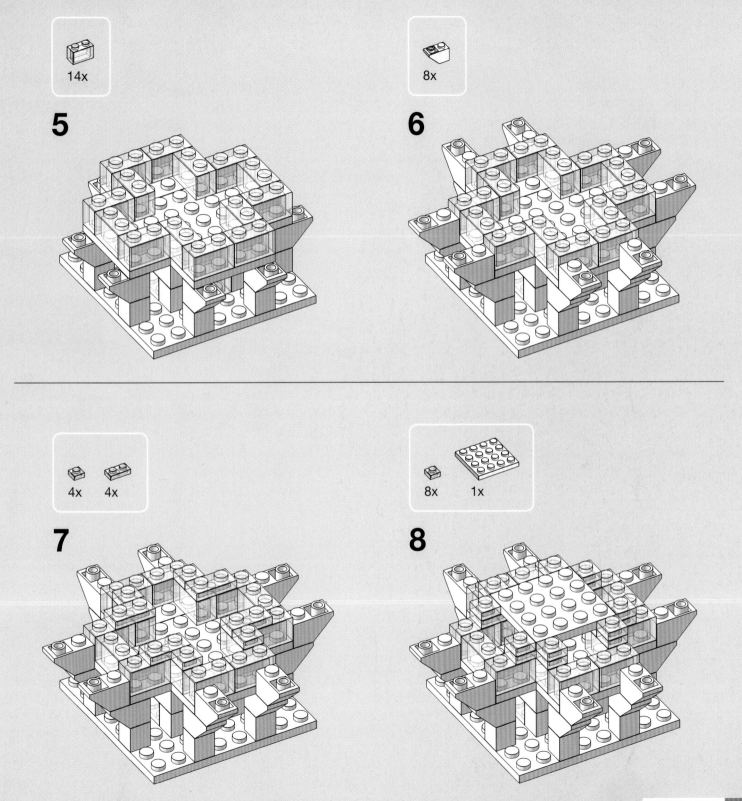

**5**

**6**

14x

8x

**7**

**8**

4x  4x

8x  1x

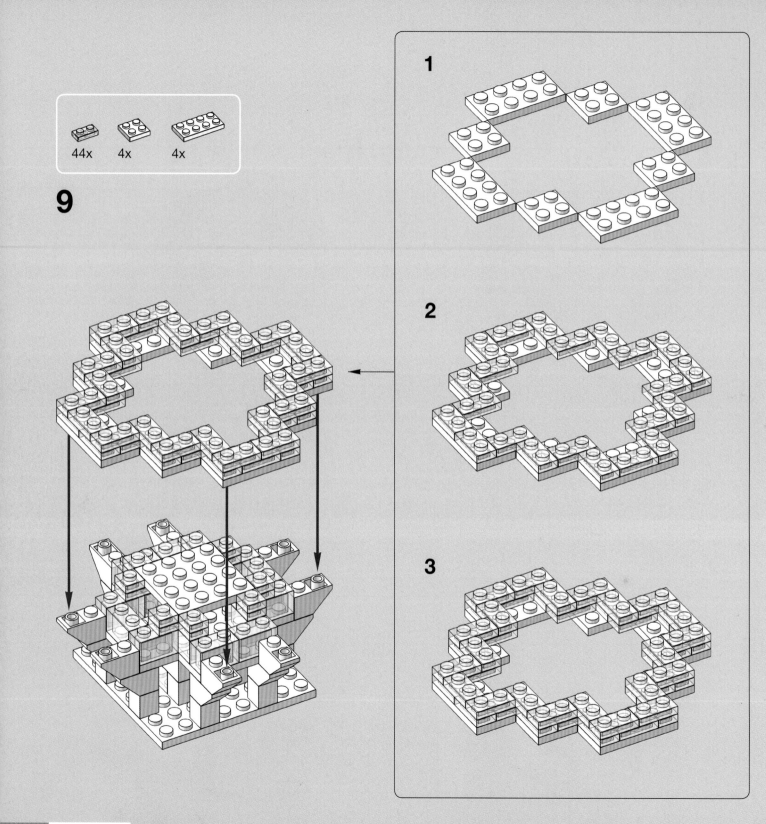

**9**

44x  4x  4x

1

2

3

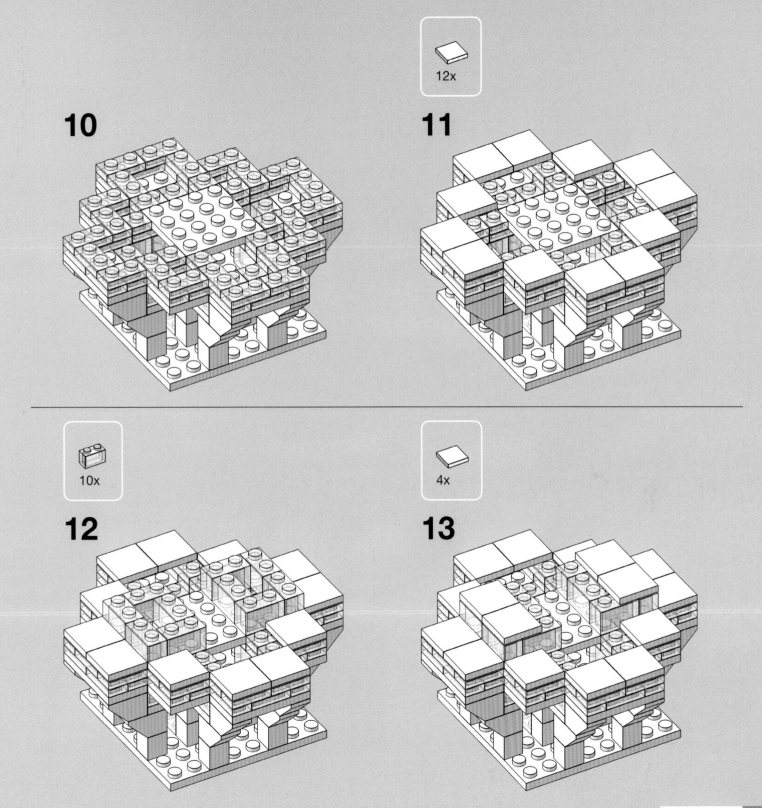

**10**

**11** 12x

**12** 10x

**13** 4x

GEISEL LIBRARY
San Diego, California, 1970,
Pereira & Associates.

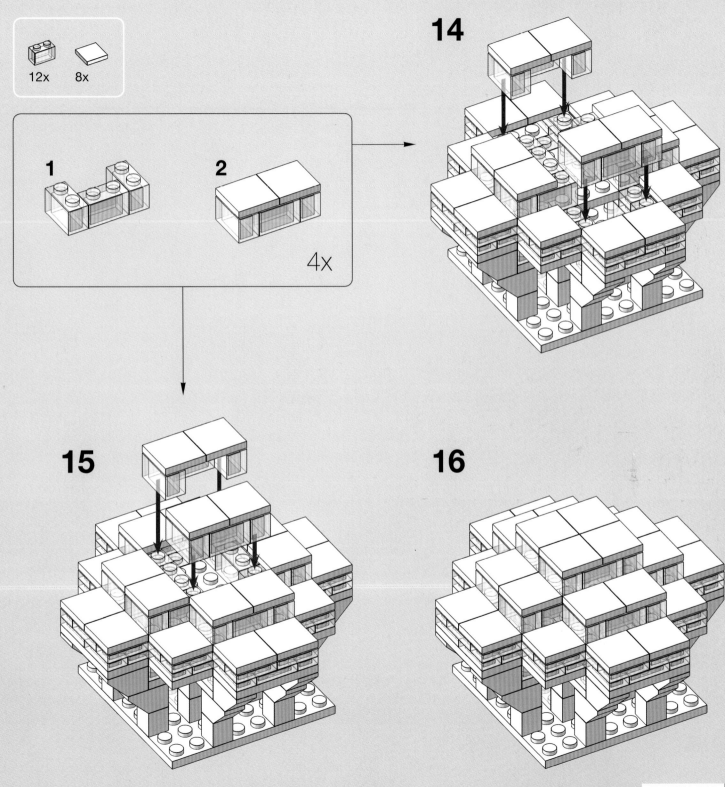

**14**

**15**

**16**

**1**

**2**

12x  8x

4x

PIAZZA D'ITALIA
New Orleans, Louisiana, 1978,
Charles Moore.

# POSTMODERN

After 40 years in the spotlight, Modernism lost some of its luster, giving way to a more decorated, historically rooted style. Postmodern architecture explores a variety of alternatives to the Modernist glass and steel boxes that were taking over the world. In response to Modernist architect Mies van der Rohe's famed statement "Less is more," Robert Venturi claimed, "Less is a bore."

BANK OF AMERICA PLAZA
Atlanta, Georgia, 1992,
Kevin Roche John Dinkeloo and Associates LLC.

SONY TOWER
New York City, New York, 1984,
Philip Johnson.

At the heart of the Postmodern movement is a desire for a more-human architecture, fueled by a strong reaction against the sterility of Modernism. Postmodern architects remix shapes, patterns, and styles from the past to create something that is both familiar and new.

Robert Venturi is most commonly cited as the first Postmodern architect. He is recognized both for his buildings and for his writings about architectural theory. He was extremely critical of the "puritanically moral language of orthodox Modern architecture." He preferred to celebrate historic forms by creating buildings designed to meet the needs of the people who use them. Vanna Venturi House (1964) is likely the first Postmodern building, which Venturi designed and built for his mother based on these principles.

By understanding how people respond to common architectural forms like arches, doorways, and columns, architects can take advantage of these subconscious meanings to design buildings that are innovative but easy to navigate. As an example, Modernist architects often leave the entrances to their buildings undecorated, but a Postmodern architect might place a decorative triangular

## MATERIALS

Most Postmodern buildings are constructed with modern elements like steel and glass, but they are often clad with more-traditional exterior materials like stone, marble, or stucco.

## LEGO PEDIMENTS

Chippendale pediment

Arched pediment

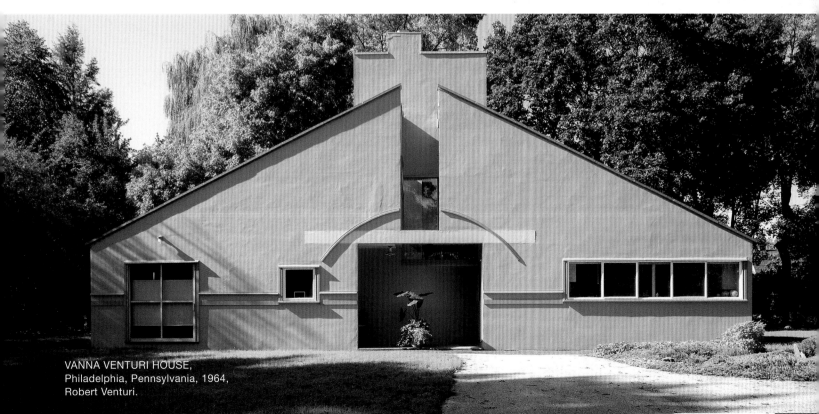

VANNA VENTURI HOUSE,
Philadelphia, Pennsylvania, 1964,
Robert Venturi.

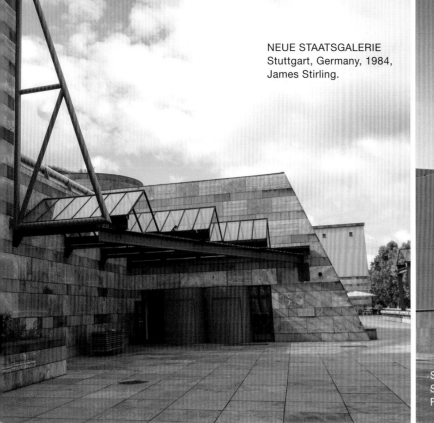

NEUE STAATSGALERIE
Stuttgart, Germany, 1984,
James Stirling.

SAN ANTONIO PUBLIC LIBRARY
San Antonio, Texas, 1995,
Ricardo Legorreta.

**LEGO BRICKS**

 Headlight bricks can be used to create a wall of tiny windows.

 Arches and curves are common in many Postmodern designs.

 Slopes are required for pitched roofs.

pediment above the door, leveraging the visual grammar of historic architecture to indicate that this must be the entrance. The Neue Staatsgalerie (1984) is a playful example of this, with simple glass pediments above the main entrance.

Another signature of Postmodern architecture is to use recognizable forms at an exaggerated scale, such as the House in Katonah (1975), which has a massive round window that dominates the front of the home. We also see distortions of common forms, like the famous Chippendale pediment on the top of the AT&T Building

(1984), now called the Sony Tower, or the neon outlines of classical forms in the Piazza d'Italia (1978).

While many Postmodern architects draw inspiration from classical forms, they explore other styles as well. Ricardo Legorreta based the San Antonio Public Library (1995) on designs from the Southwest. The Postmodern movement isn't limited to Western architecture: Taipei 101 (2004), one of the tallest buildings in the world, has a Postmodern design inspired by the pagoda, a tiered tower common in traditional Asian architecture.

Critics of the style suggest that Postmodern architects are simply exploiting social or historical cues for the benefit of corporate brands. For example, a building might include a facade with decorative columns because they are a subconscious symbol of strength. Of course, the same could be said for the many corporations that embraced Modernism just 30 years earlier. Several iconic Postmodern buildings have become central to the corporate brands they represent, such as the Transamerica Pyramid (1972).

## POSTMODERN IN LEGO

Since many Postmodern buildings utilize simplified representations of historical design elements, capturing Postmodern architecture using LEGO bricks can be a challenge. The very process of reducing a large building into a small-scale LEGO model is similar to the way that Postmodern architects reduce historical architectural elements to their simplest forms. This is why LEGO re-creations of any architectural style will have a slightly Postmodern appearance. The models in this chapter are based on the strong geometric designs that are unique to this style.

### LEGO COLORS

- Light bluish grey
- Tan
- Dark orange
- Dark red
- Medium blue
- Sand green
- Trans light blue

HOUSE IN KATONAH
Katonah, New York, 1975,
Venturi, Scott Brown and Associates.

# POSTMODERN LEGO MODELS

**DENVER PUBLIC LIBRARY**
Denver, Colorado, 1995, Michael Graves.
LEGO model by Imagine Rigney.

**CITY RESTAURANT**
LEGO model by Brian and Jason Lyles.

**CHILI'S RESTAURANT**
LEGO model by Brian and Jason Lyles.

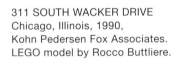

311 SOUTH WACKER DRIVE
Chicago, Illinois, 1990,
Kohn Pedersen Fox Associates.
LEGO model by Rocco Buttliere.

TAIPEI 101
Taipei, Taiwan, 2004,
C.Y. Lee & Partners.
LEGO model by Spencer Rezkalla.

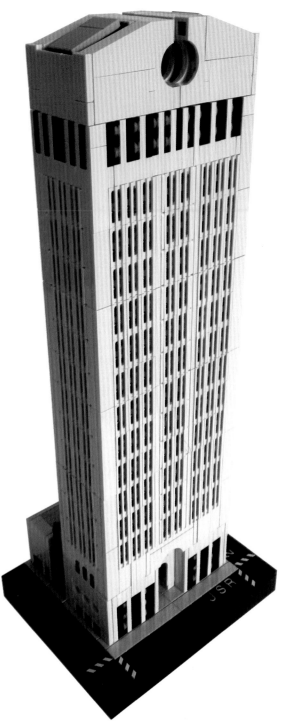

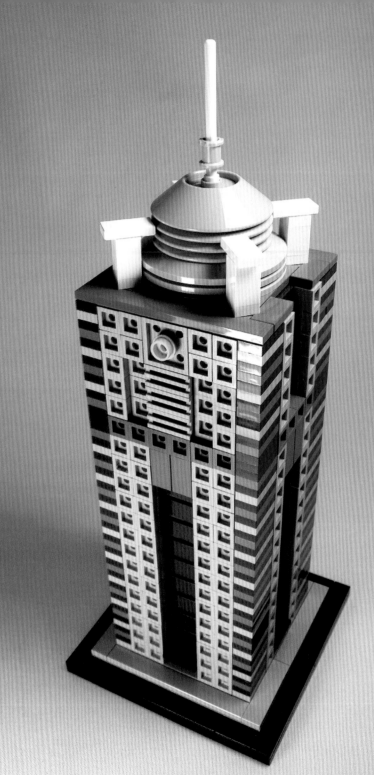

SONY TOWER
New York City, New York, 1984, Philip Johnson and John Burgee.
LEGO model by Spencer Rezkalla.

CHINA MERCHANTS TOWER
Shanghai, China, 1995, Simon Kwan & Associates Ltd.
LEGO model by Jens Ohrndorf.

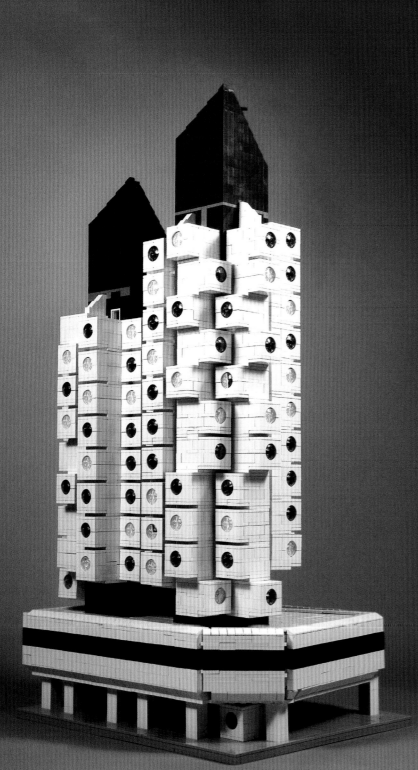

**NAKAGIN CAPSULE TOWER**
Tokyo, Japan, 1972, Kisho Kurokawa.
LEGO model by Matthew Allum and his daughters Akemie and Alleke.

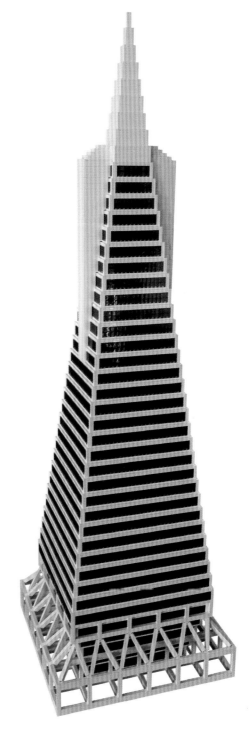

**TRANSAMERICA PYRAMID**
San Francisco, California, 1972, William Pereira.
LEGO model by Adam Reed Tucker.

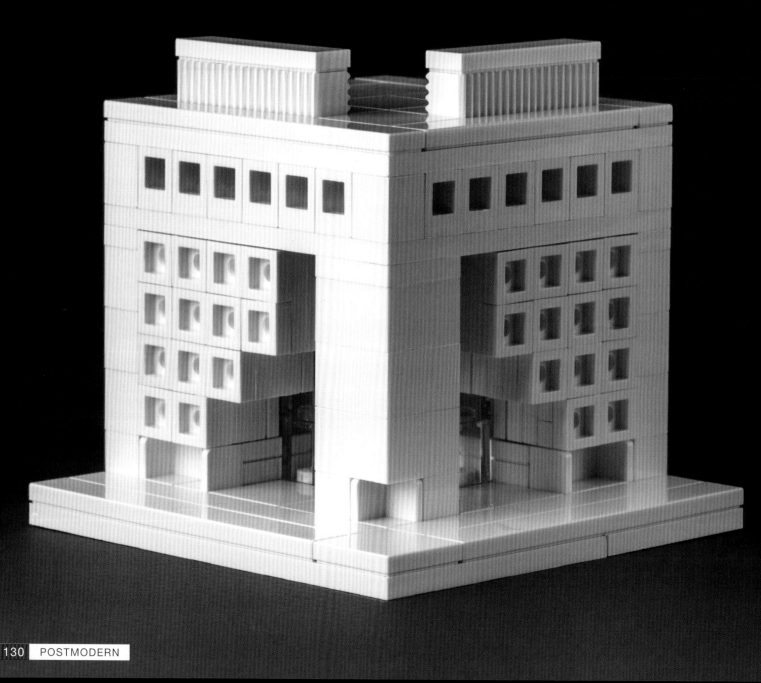

# OFFICE BUILDING

Based on Ransila I (1990), an office building in Switzerland by architect Mario Botta, this model features square windows placed on a strict grid and a broken facade punctuated by a single column in the front.

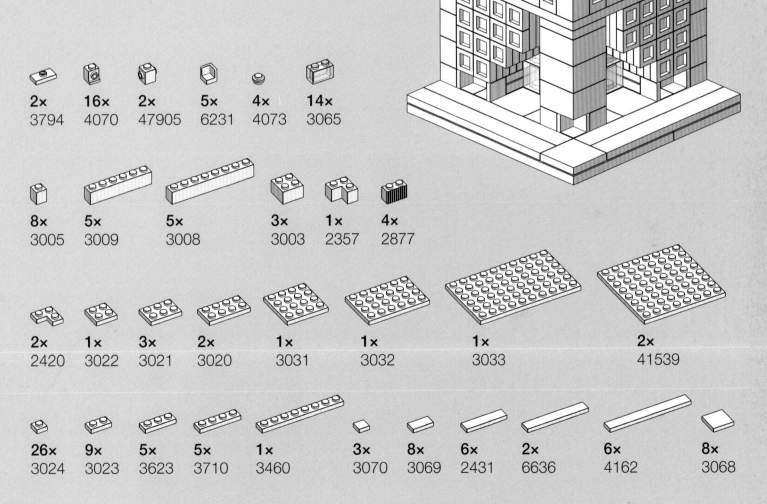

| | | | | | |
|---|---|---|---|---|---|
| **2x** 3794 | **16x** 4070 | **2x** 47905 | **5x** 6231 | **4x** 4073 | **14x** 3065 |

| | | | | | |
|---|---|---|---|---|---|
| **8x** 3005 | **5x** 3009 | **5x** 3008 | **3x** 3003 | **1x** 2357 | **4x** 2877 |

| | | | | | | | |
|---|---|---|---|---|---|---|---|
| **2x** 2420 | **1x** 3022 | **3x** 3021 | **2x** 3020 | **1x** 3031 | **1x** 3032 | **1x** 3033 | **2x** 41539 |

| | | | | | | | | | | |
|---|---|---|---|---|---|---|---|---|---|---|
| **26x** 3024 | **9x** 3023 | **5x** 3623 | **5x** 3710 | **1x** 3460 | **3x** 3070 | **8x** 3069 | **6x** 2431 | **2x** 6636 | **6x** 4162 | **8x** 3068 |

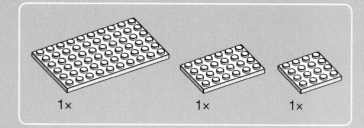

**1**

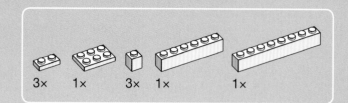

**2**

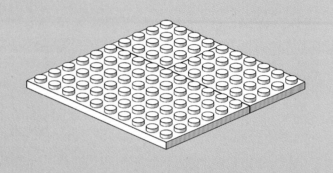

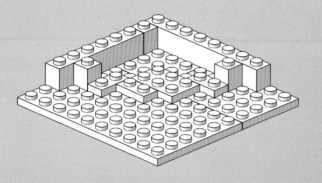

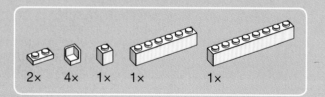

**3**

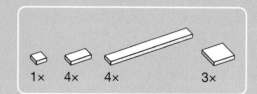

**4**

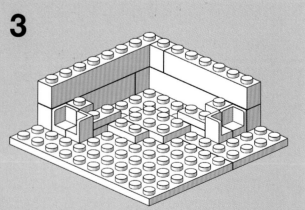

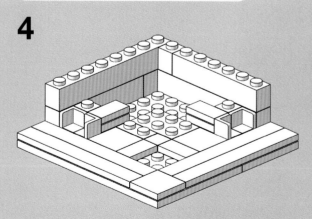

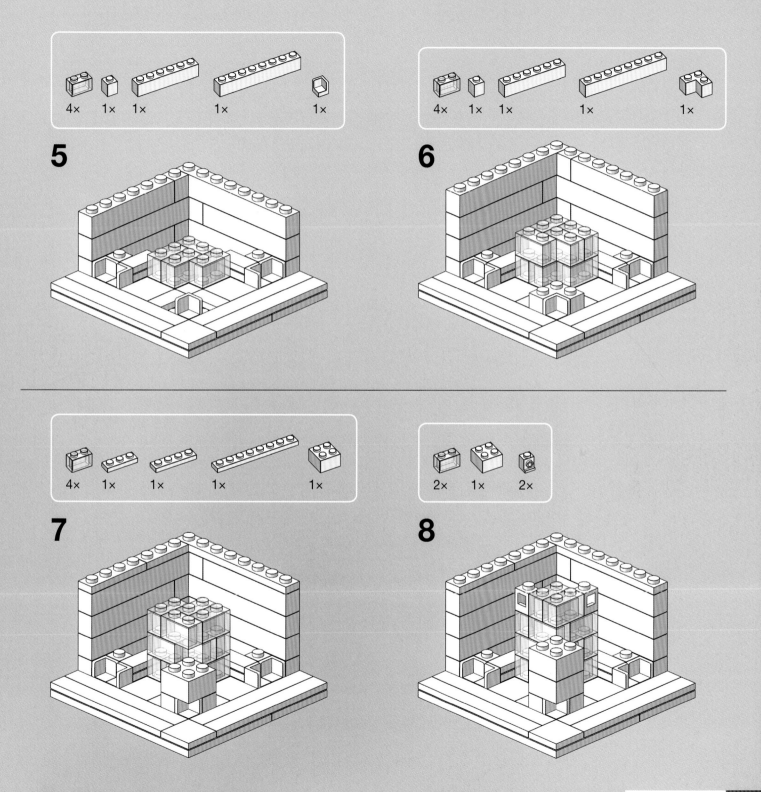

**5**

4× 1× 1× 1× 1×

**6**

4× 1× 1× 1× 1×

**7**

4× 1× 1× 1× 1×

**8**

2× 1× 2×

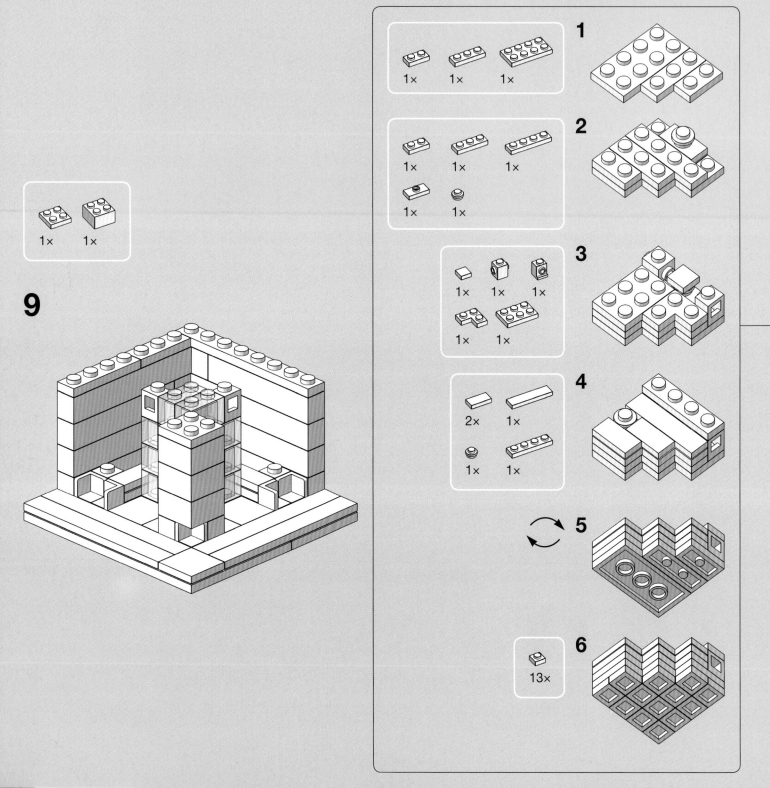

**9**

1
1x 1x 1x

2
1x 1x 1x
1x 1x

3
1x 1x 1x
1x 1x

4
2x 1x
1x 1x

5

6
13x

1x 1x

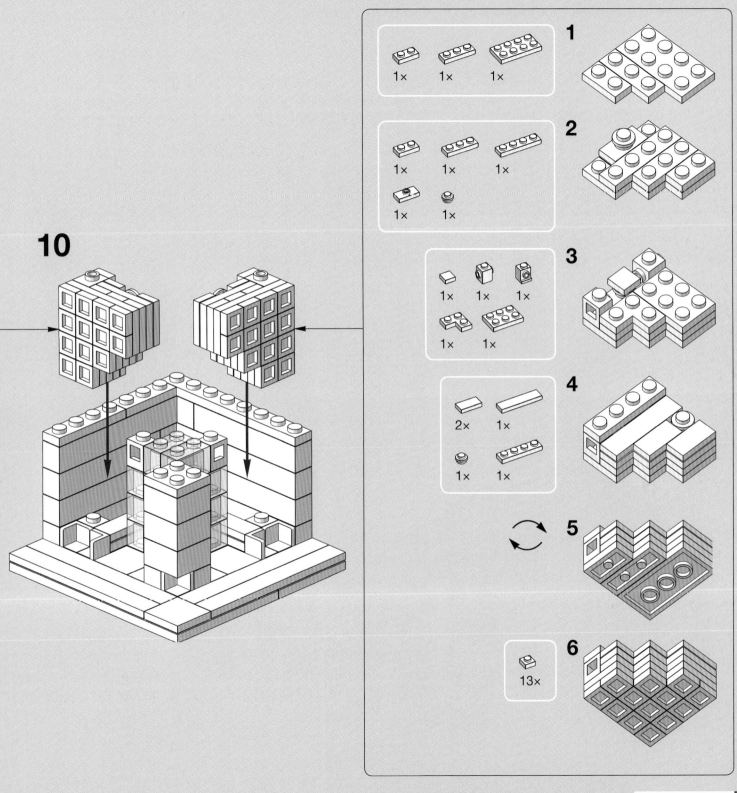

**10**

1

1x  1x  1x

2

1x  1x  1x
1x  1x

3

1x  1x  1x
1x  1x

4

2x  1x
1x  1x

5

6

13x

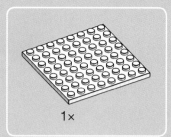

**11**

1×

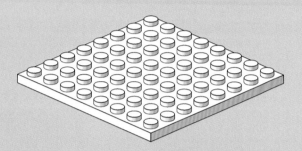

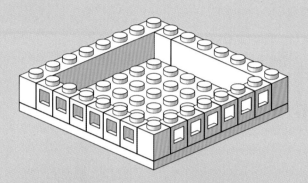

**12**

2× 1× 1× 12×

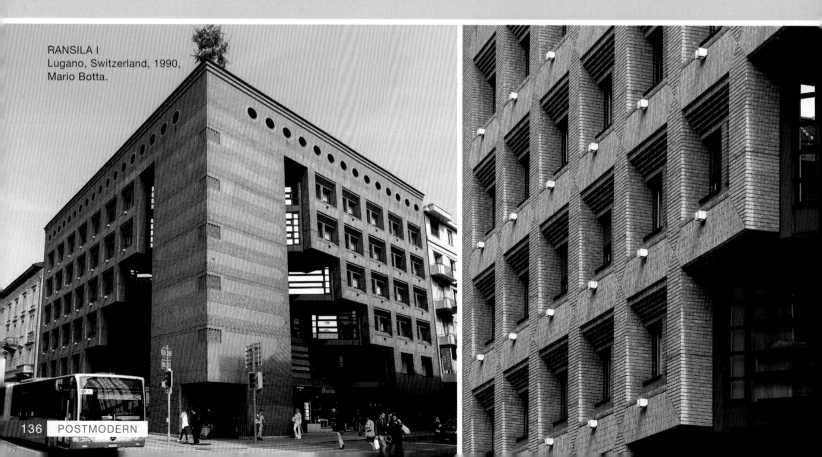

RANSILA I
Lugano, Switzerland, 1990,
Mario Botta.

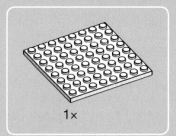

**13**

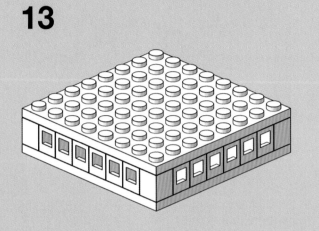

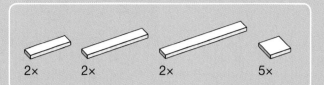

**14**

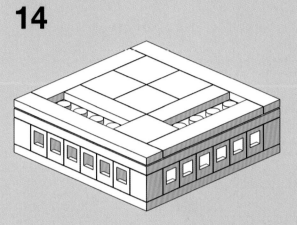

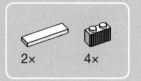

**15**

**16**

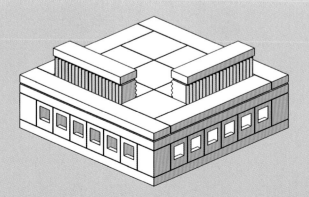

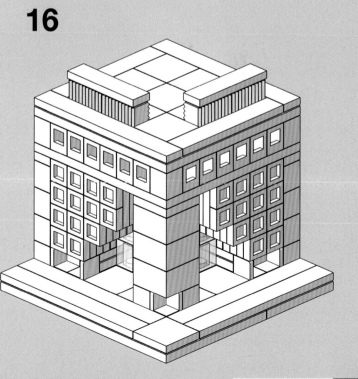

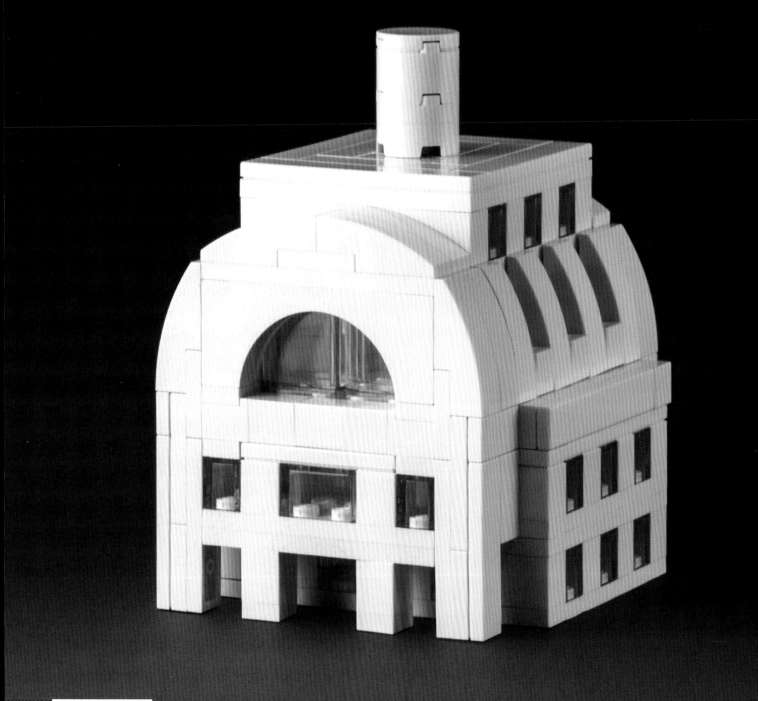

# UNIVERSITY BUILDING

This model is inspired by the Engineering Research Center (1995) in Cincinnati, Ohio, by architect Michael Graves. Prominent features include the arched roof, which dominates the design, and blocky columns on the front facade.

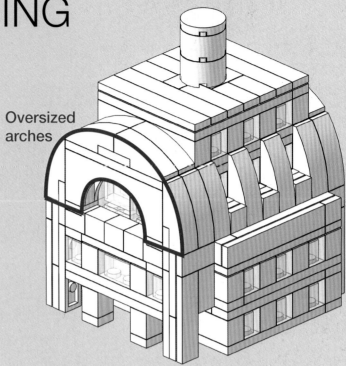

Oversized arches

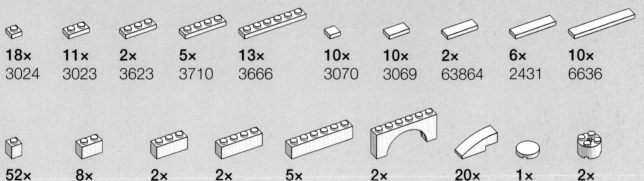

| | | | | |
|---|---|---|---|---|
| **12×** 3024 | **43×** 3065 | **8×** 87552 | **2×** 3794 | **4×** 4070 |

| | | | | | | | | | |
|---|---|---|---|---|---|---|---|---|---|
| **18×** 3024 | **11×** 3023 | **2×** 3623 | **5×** 3710 | **13×** 3666 | **10×** 3070 | **10×** 3069 | **2×** 63864 | **6×** 2431 | **10×** 6636 |

| | | | | | | | | |
|---|---|---|---|---|---|---|---|---|
| **52×** 3005 | **8×** 3004 | **2×** 3622 | **2×** 3010 | **5×** 3009 | **2×** 3307 | **20×** 50950 | **1×** 4150 | **2×** 3941 |

| | | | | | | |
|---|---|---|---|---|---|---|
| **1×** 3022 | **2×** 3021 | **2×** 3020 | **5×** 3795 | **5×** 3958 | **1×** 3033 | **1×** 4477 |

**1**

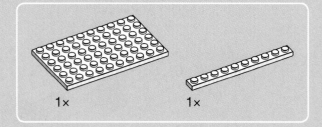

1×      1×

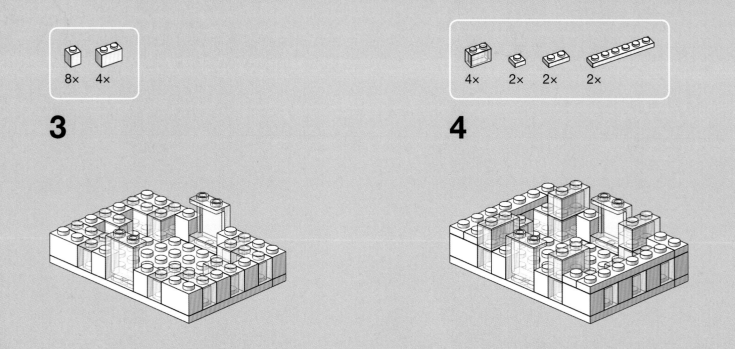

**2**

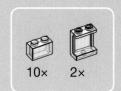

10×      2×

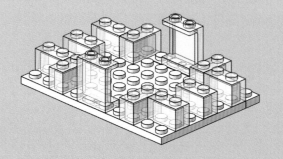

**3**

8×      4×

**4**

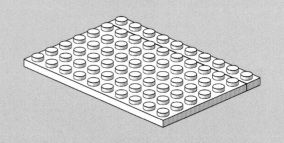

4×      2×      2×      2×

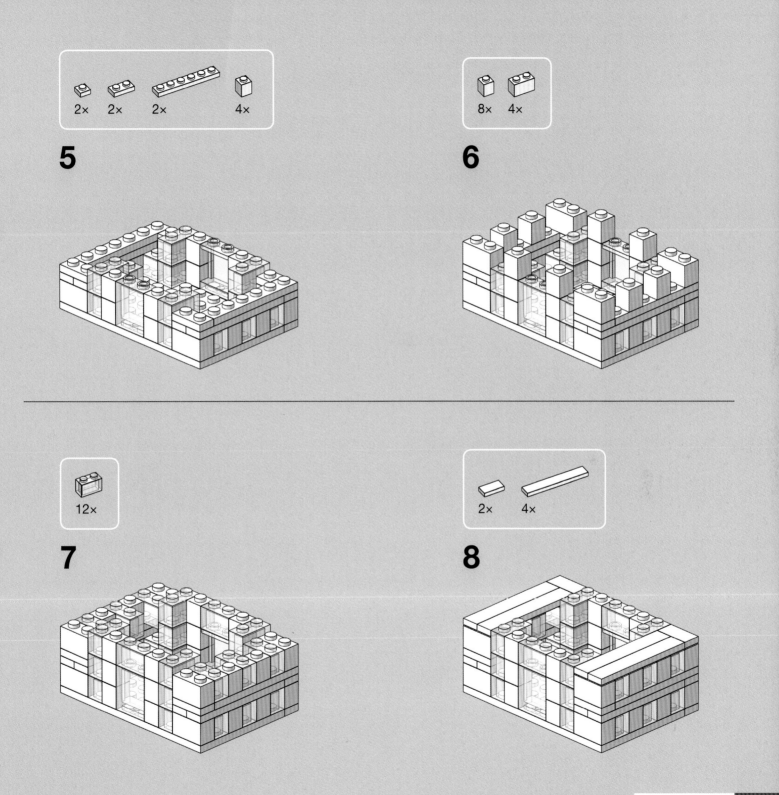

**5**

**6**

2× 2× 2× 4×

8× 4×

**7**

**8**

12×

2× 4×

**9**

**10**

**11**

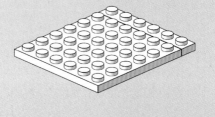

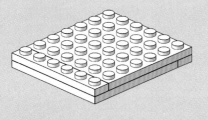

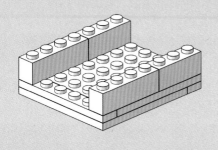

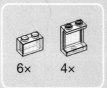

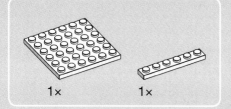

**12**

**13**

**14**

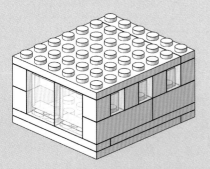

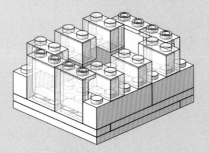

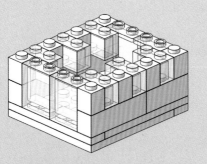

**15**

**16**

**17**

**18**

**19**

**20**

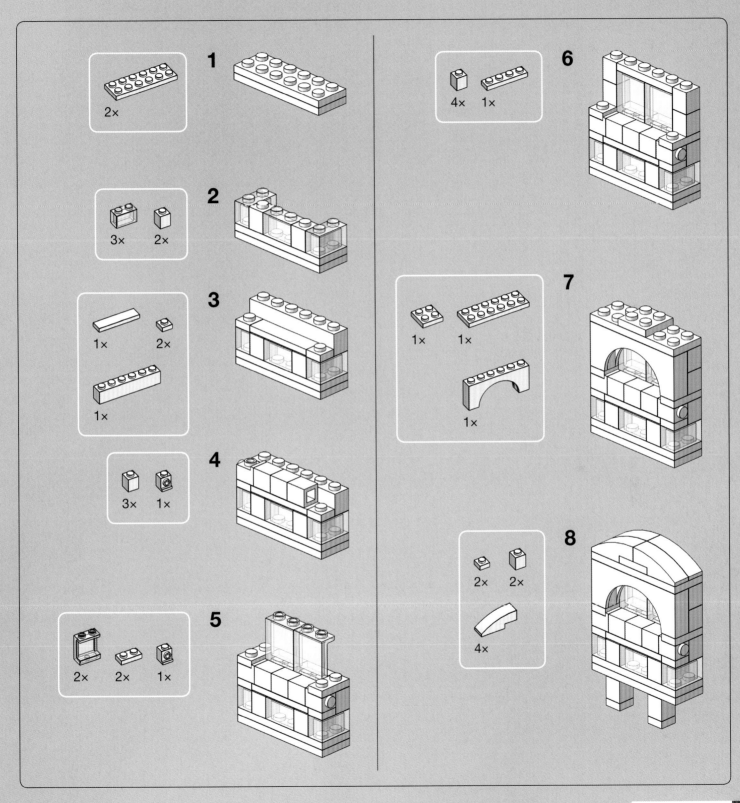

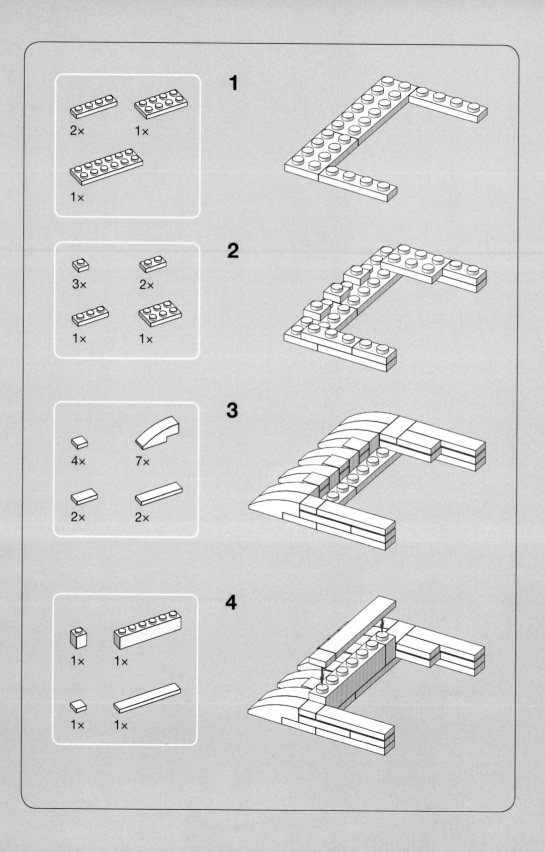

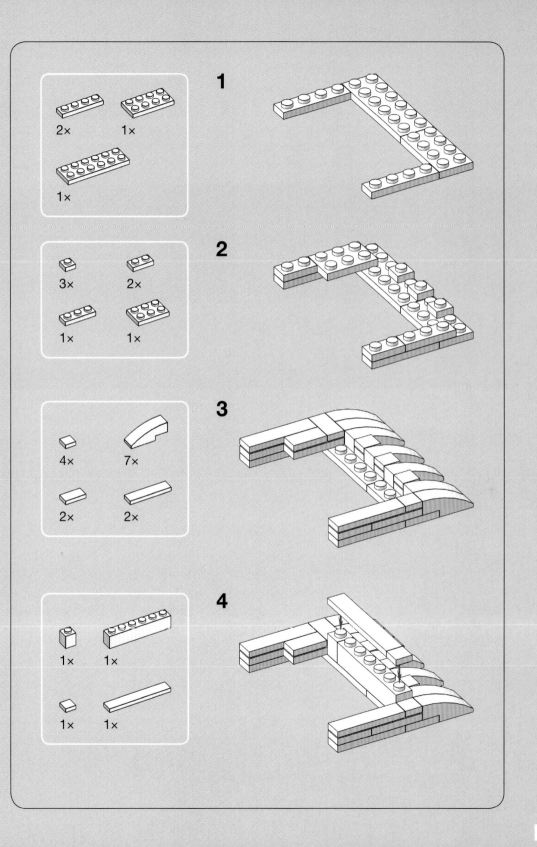

ENGINEERING RESEARCH CENTER
Cincinnati, Ohio, 1995,
Michael Graves.

**21**

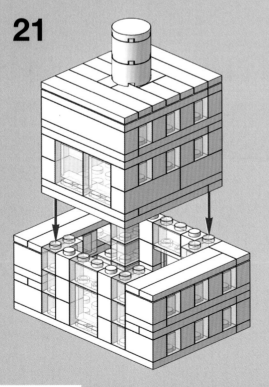

**22**

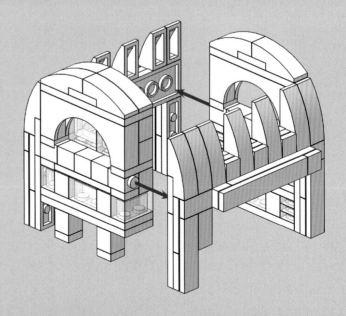

**23**

**24**

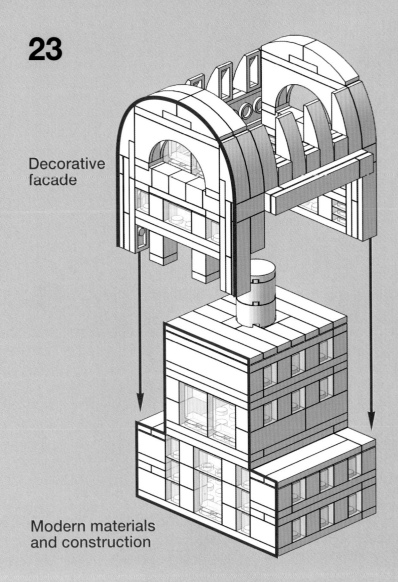

Decorative
facade

Modern materials
and construction

The model is built in two stages. A decorative
facade covers a simple modern core. Most
Postmodern buildings use cost-saving modern
construction techniques and materials despite
a classically inspired exterior.

# HIGH-TECH

The diverse architectural forms of
the last 30 years have only become
possible with the development
of advanced computer modeling
software. Computer-aided design
and high-tech fabrication methods
have allowed architects to create
buildings with shocking, abstract
sculptural forms.

MICHAEL LEE-CHIN CRYSTAL, ROYAL ONTARIO MUSEUM
Toronto, Canada, 2007,
Daniel Libeskind.

SYDNEY OPERA HOUSE
Sydney, Australia, 1973,
Jørn Utzon.

GUGGENHEIM MUSEUM BILBAO
Bilbao, Spain, 1997,
Frank Gehry.

The iconic shell-shaped Sydney Opera House (1973) is one of the first buildings where computers were used throughout the design process, ushering in a new High-Tech style. Primitive computer models helped the design team calculate the structure needed to support the huge concrete shells and provided the precise measurements required to ensure that each rib of the shells lined up seamlessly.

In 1997, architecture with complex curved forms reached a new level with the Guggenheim Museum Bilbao by Frank Gehry. This building's popularity made Gehry into a celebrity architect, or "starchitect." He has built similar buildings all over the world, including the Walt Disney Concert Hall (2003) in Los Angeles.

We see similar abstract forms but with sharp, chiseled angles in the Michael Lee-Chin Crystal (2007), the Royal Ontario Museum's main entrance. It is an aggressive High-Tech design by Daniel Libeskind that is made all the more shocking by being grafted onto the classically designed museum.

This style is sometimes called *Deconstructivism*, because the basic shapes of the buildings have been visibly

## MATERIALS

High-Tech buildings employ a wide range of materials, including advanced plastics, machine-cut plywood, concrete, and lots of glass and steel. The Guggenheim Museum Bilbao is covered in titanium panels that are just one-third of a millimeter thick!

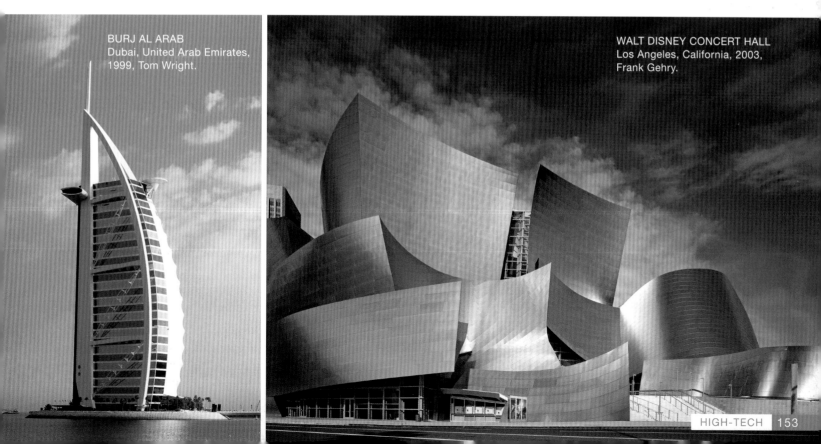

BURJ AL ARAB
Dubai, United Arab Emirates, 1999, Tom Wright.

WALT DISNEY CONCERT HALL
Los Angeles, California, 2003, Frank Gehry.

## LEGO BRICKS

Technic parts can be used to re-create structural elements of a building.

Wedges and curved parts can approximate the curves of a complex sculptural form.

Hoses can be bent into curved forms and attached with clips.

disassembled, broken, and crumpled, with the structural supports usually hidden from view.

At the other extreme is the Centre Georges Pompidou (1977), which celebrates the structure and functions of the building by putting all the guts of the building on the exterior instead of trying to hide them on the inside. It's an inside-out building! This is among the first of many High-Tech buildings to have a rectangular form harking back to Modernism, but with a more playful design. Other examples of this High-Tech Modernism include the HSBC Building (1985) by Norman Foster and the Bank of China Tower (1990) by I.M. Pei.

A few architects have blended High-Tech Modernism and Deconstructivism

into a single building where the support structure is the focus of the design. The most prominent examples are the work of Santiago Calatrava, a structural engineer, architect, and sculptor who has designed bridges and buildings such as the Reggio Emilia AV Mediopadana (2013), which has a soaring bridge-like structure. The Burj Al Arab (1999), designed by Tom Wright, is another iconic example of this blended style; the hotel's exterior is sleek and curvy but still shows off the diagonal bracing in the final design.

In some extreme cases, High-Tech architects are literally allowing the computer to take over parts of the design process. Architects describe the shape they want to achieve and then rely on computer algorithms to determine the most efficient way to construct it. In the future, computers might be able to design a whole building, but will they be able to compete with the creative genius of a great architect?

## HIGH-TECH IN LEGO

LEGO, with its rectangular shapes and predictable proportions, is not the ideal medium for capturing the curved forms common in Deconstructivist designs like those by Frank Gehry. That said, you can approximate curves in large-scale models using basic bricks, or look for curved pieces such as those normally used for an airplane nose.

Some of the more rectangular High-Tech buildings are more practical to construct with LEGO. You may be able to build them using basic LEGO bricks, or use Technic liftarms, axles, and pins to create advanced structural engineering forms, as well as building at unusual angles.

**LEGO COLORS**

- White
- Light bluish grey
- Black
- Red
- Orange
- Lime
- Medium blue
- Trans light blue
- Trans clear

REGGIO EMILIA AV MEDIOPADANA
Emilia-Romagna, Italy, 2013,
Santiago Calatrava.

# HIGH-TECH LEGO MODELS

**BURJ AL ARAB**
Dubai, United Arab Emirates, 1999, Tom Wright.
LEGO model by Spencer Rezkalla.

**BANK OF CHINA TOWER**
Hong Kong, 1990, I.M. Pei & Partners.
LEGO model by Spencer Rezkalla.

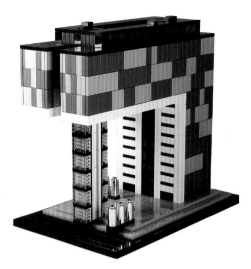

**KRANHAUS SÜD**
Cologne, Germany, 2011, Alfons Linster and Hadi Teherani.
LEGO model by Jens Ohrndorf.

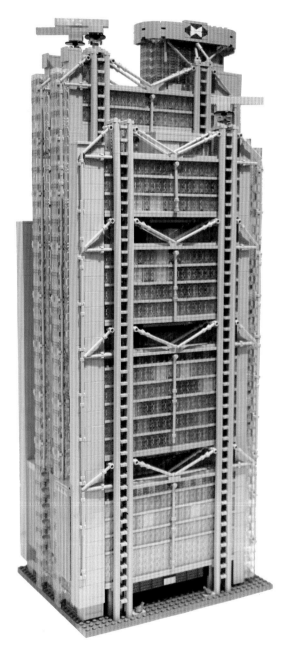

**HSBC BUILDING**
Hong Kong, 1985, Foster + Partners.
LEGO model by Jared Chan.

**AQUA**
Chicago, Illinois, 2009, Jeanne Gang.
LEGO model by Rocco Buttliere.

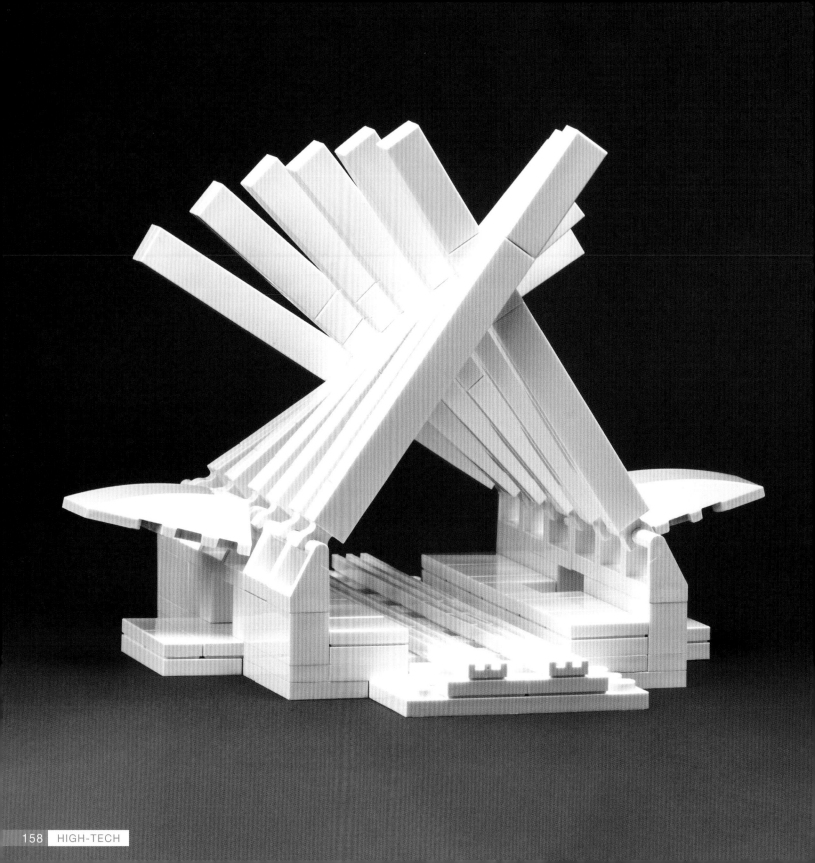

# TRAIN STATION

This High-Tech train station has a visible
structure inspired by several buildings
designed by architect Santiago Calatrava.

This is an example of parametric architecture
where each section of the roof crosses at a
lower point than the beam in front of it. This
approximates a curved roof using straight
beams.

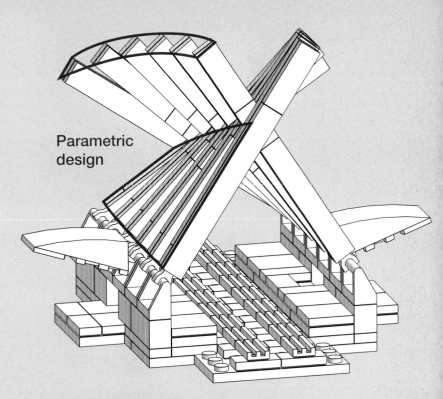

Parametric
design

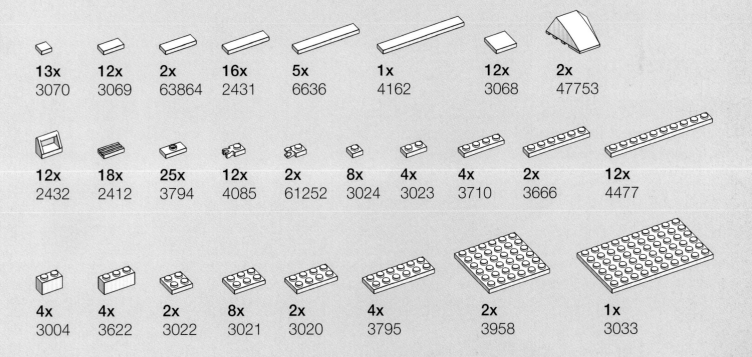

| 13x | 12x | 2x | 16x | 5x | 1x | 12x | 2x |
|---|---|---|---|---|---|---|---|
| 3070 | 3069 | 63864 | 2431 | 6636 | 4162 | 3068 | 47753 |

| 12x | 18x | 25x | 12x | 2x | 8x | 4x | 4x | 2x | 12x |
|---|---|---|---|---|---|---|---|---|---|
| 2432 | 2412 | 3794 | 4085 | 61252 | 3024 | 3023 | 3710 | 3666 | 4477 |

| 4x | 4x | 2x | 8x | 2x | 4x | 2x | 1x |
|---|---|---|---|---|---|---|---|
| 3004 | 3622 | 3022 | 3021 | 3020 | 3795 | 3958 | 3033 |

**1**

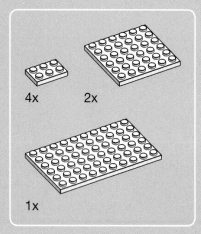

4x  2x

1x

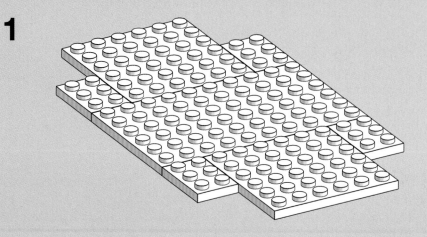

**2**

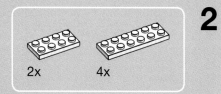

2x  4x

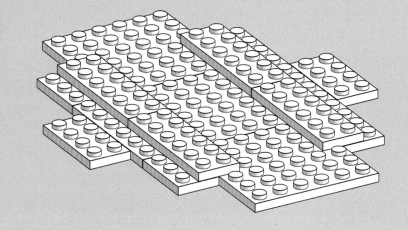

**3**

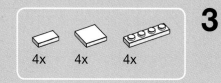

4x  4x  4x

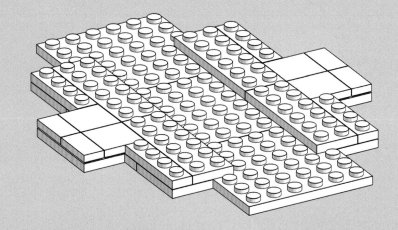

**4**

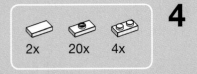

2x    20x    4x

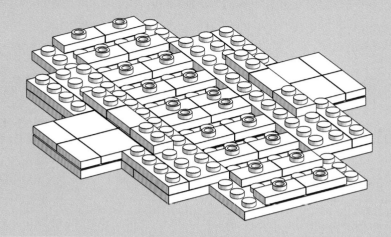

**5**

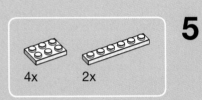

4x    2x

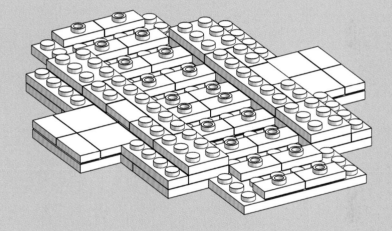

**6**

18x

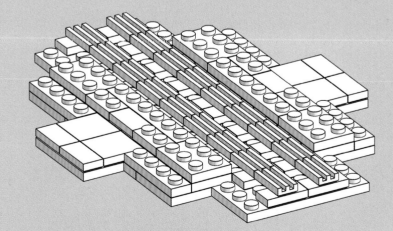

**7**

6x  8x

**8**

4x  4x

**9**

12x

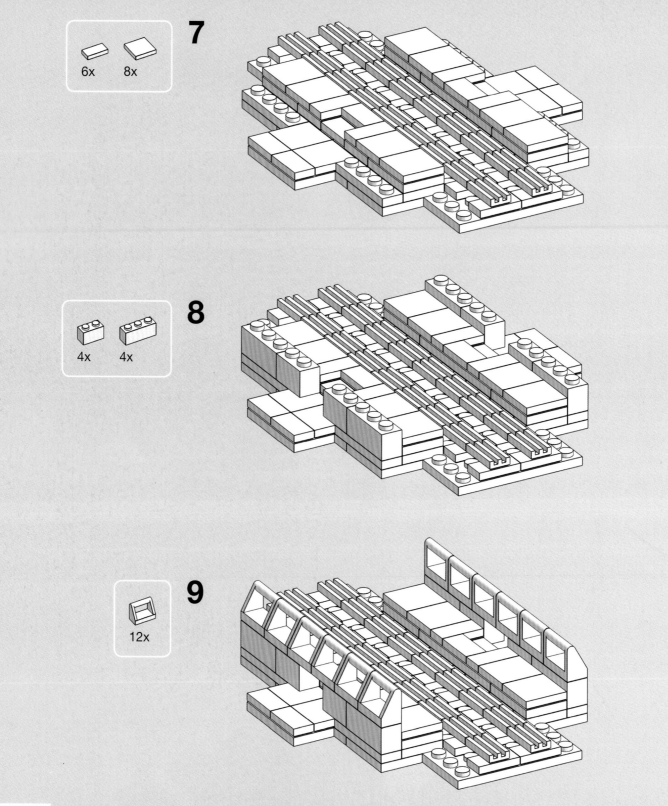

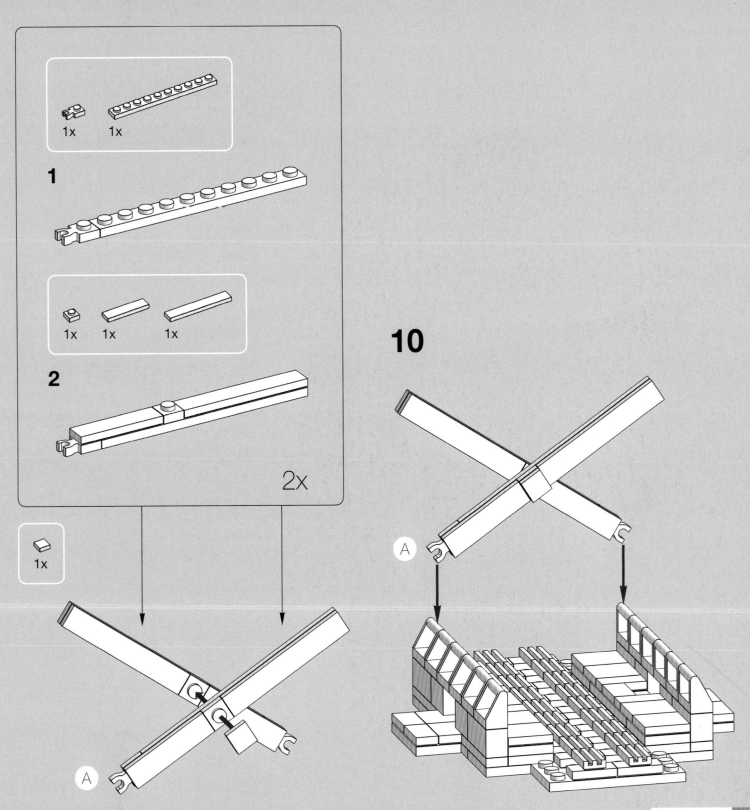

**1**

**2**

2x

1x

**10**

A

A

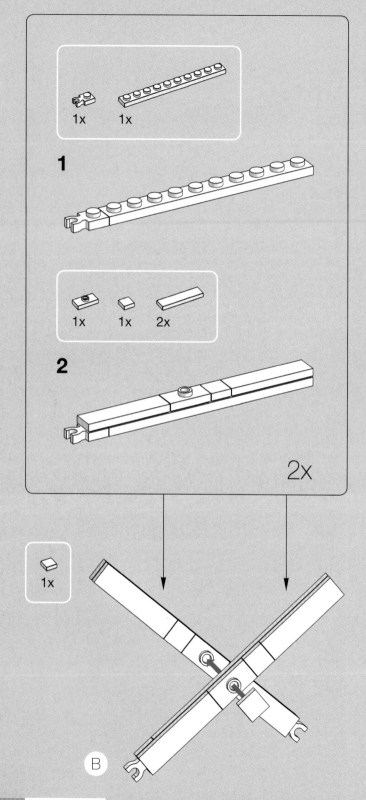

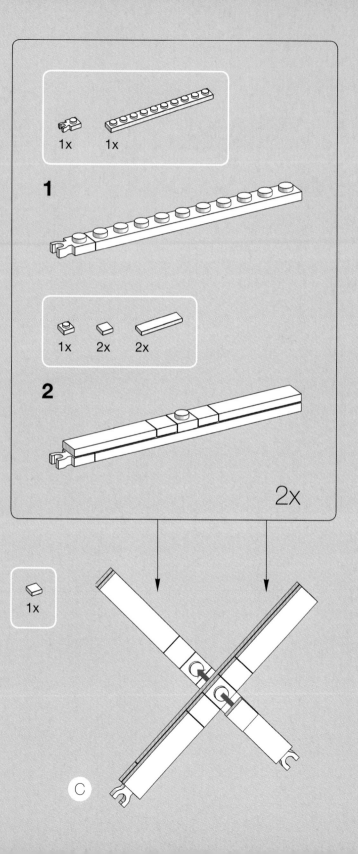

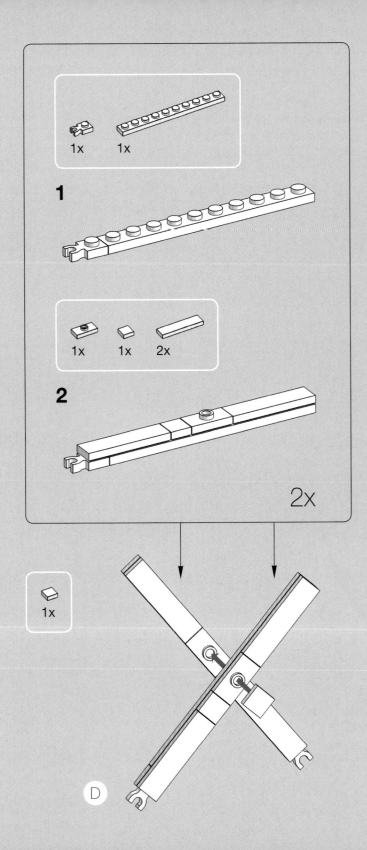

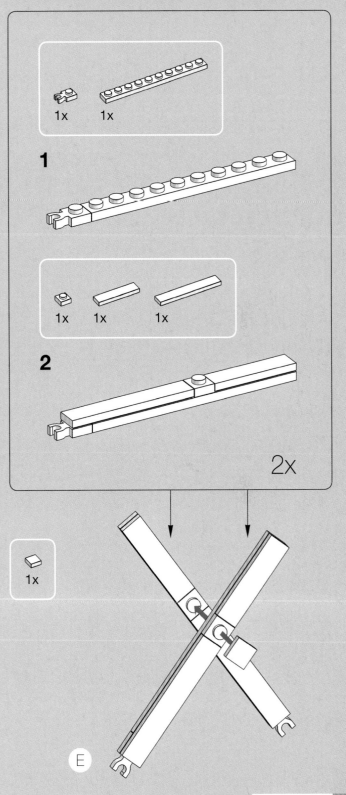

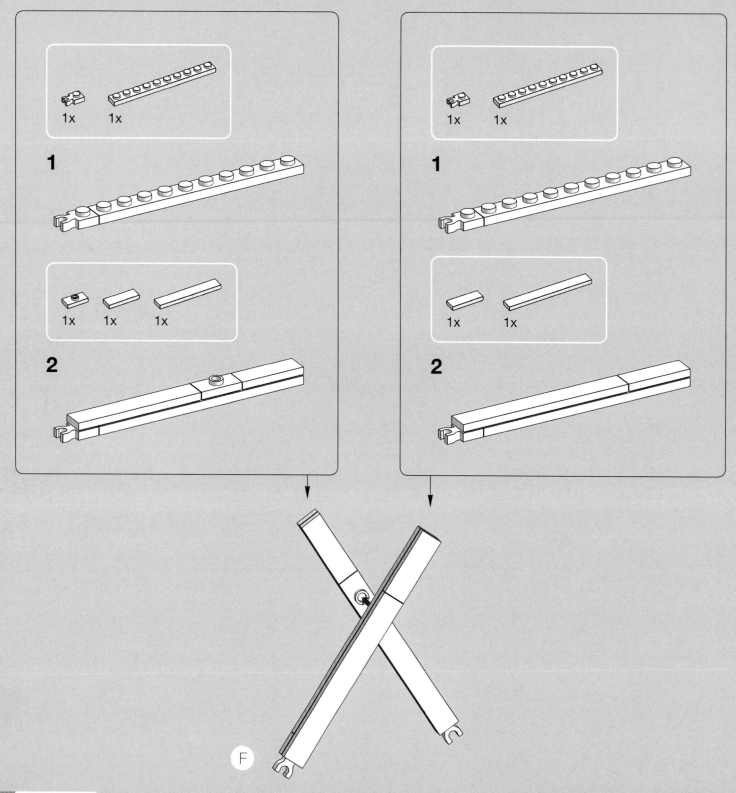

**11**

F

E

D

C

B

A

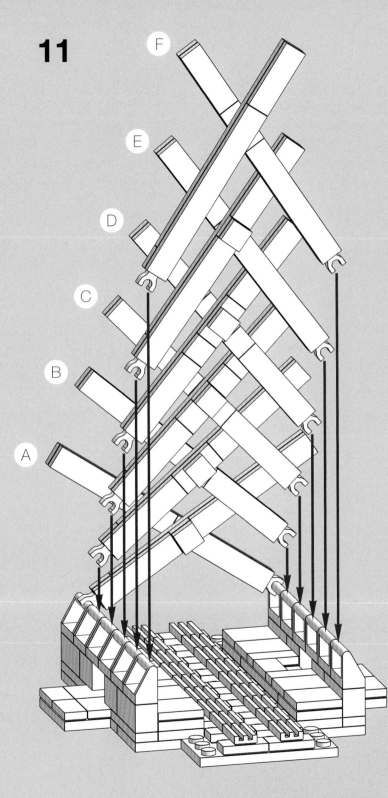

**12**

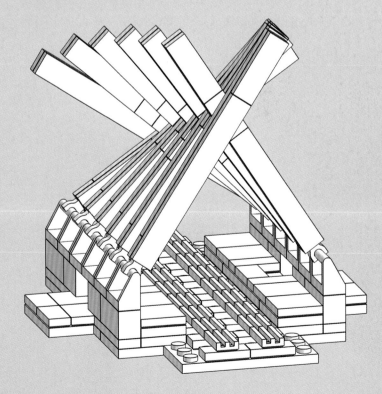

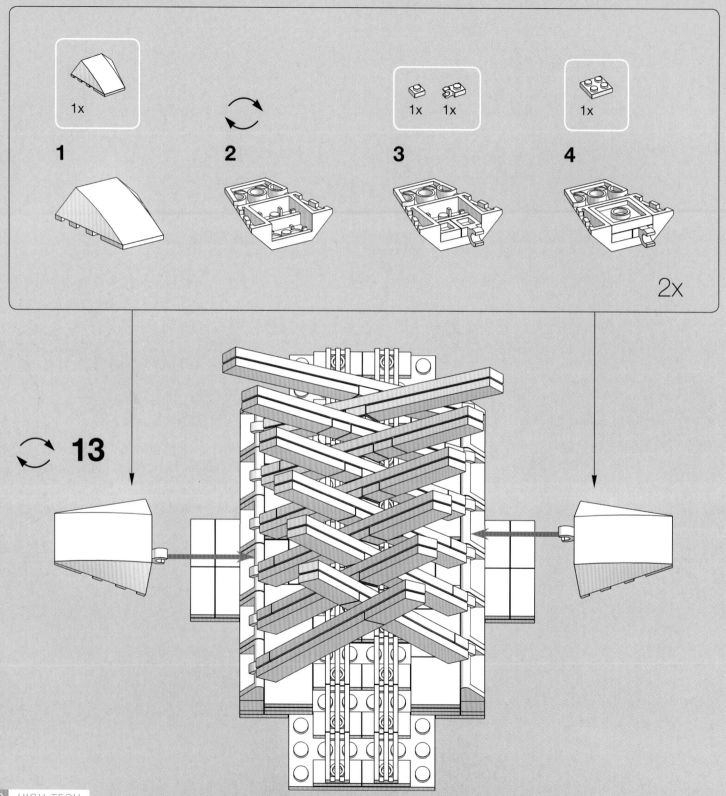

**14**

QUADRACCI PAVILION, MILWAUKEE ART MUSEUM
Milwaukee, Wisconsin, 2001,
Santiago Calatrava.

WINGSPREAD, in progress.
LEGO model by Jameson Gagnepain.

# BUILDER'S GUIDE

Now it's your turn to create your own LEGO architecture!

Whether you want to create a model of your dream home or re-create your favorite building, here are some tips to get started.

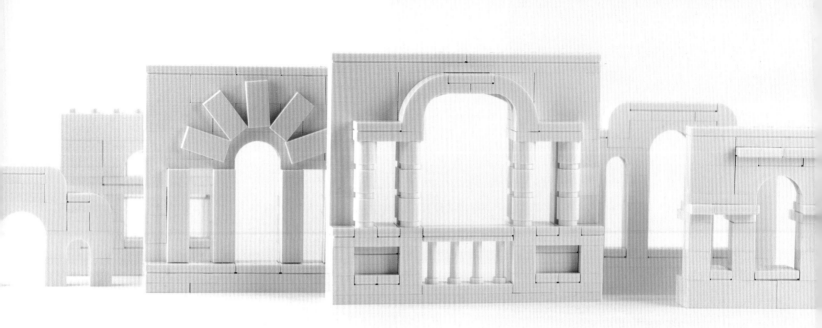

Experimenting with many different ways to build Palladian windows.

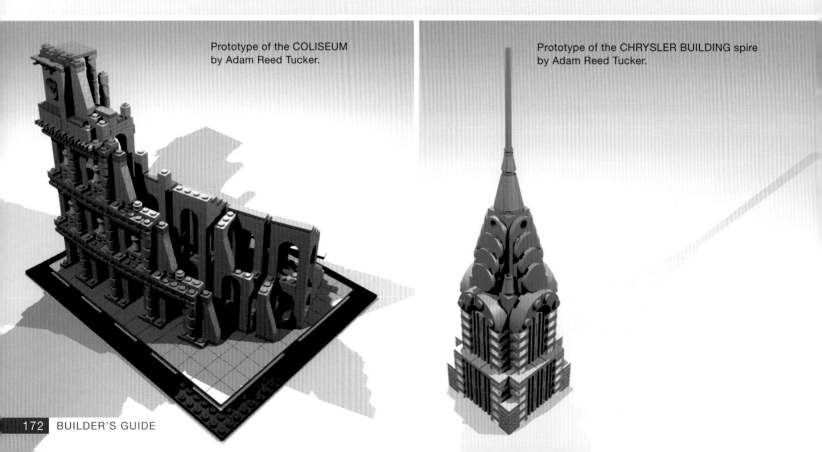

Prototype of the COLISEUM
by Adam Reed Tucker.

Prototype of the CHRYSLER BUILDING spire
by Adam Reed Tucker.

# IDEAS

With so many amazing buildings around the world, how do you decide which one to re-create with LEGO? A good way to start is to pick an architectural style you like or your favorite architect. Look for books or websites that include many different buildings so you can find something that you're excited to build. Documentary videos are another great resource because they allow you to see buildings from multiple perspectives.

You can always look around your city for inspiration, too. Jameson Gagnepain likes to build models of buildings near his home: "It's great to show people real buildings that they recognize. That really gets the attention of people who don't normally appreciate LEGO."

When you have a specific building in mind, it's time to do some research. Collecting photographs from several different angles will help you capture the most important details in your model. You may be able to find 3D models of a building in Google Street View, or detailed floor plans to help you understand the building better. You might even be able to visit the building—many historic or notable buildings offer tours.

## DESIGN YOUR OWN BUILDING

Maybe you would rather build a model of your dream home or design the perfect skyscraper. Many architects build models to explore interesting new designs, and you can too! Models let architects improve a building before it's constructed.

Even if you decide to construct a LEGO building of your own design, you'll want to do some research. Once you've picked your favorite architectural style, you can study many different buildings to find interesting architectural details that you want to include in your design. Create a scrapbook of favorite buildings and architectural features, capture ideas in a sketchbook, or build a rough model using LEGO bricks. Don't feel like you need to stick with just one style, either. Architects have been combining elements from different architectural styles for years, and you can too. This approach is called *eclecticism*, and it was especially popular in the late 1800s.

**BUILDER PROFILE:
JAMESON GAGNEPAIN**

Jameson is a founding member and the vice president of KLUG, the LEGO users group in Kenosha, Wisconsin. The Modular Buildings series got him excited about building LEGO architecture models. He even had a LEGO-themed wedding, where the guests had turned the LEGO centerpieces into towers and spaceships by the end of the night.

Jameson loves to build LEGO models of the buildings in his community. This includes a number of buildings by Frank Lloyd Wright, which Jameson has re-created as large models with intricate details and advanced building techniques. His latest project is a sprawling 5×5-foot LEGO re-creation of Wright's Wingspread.

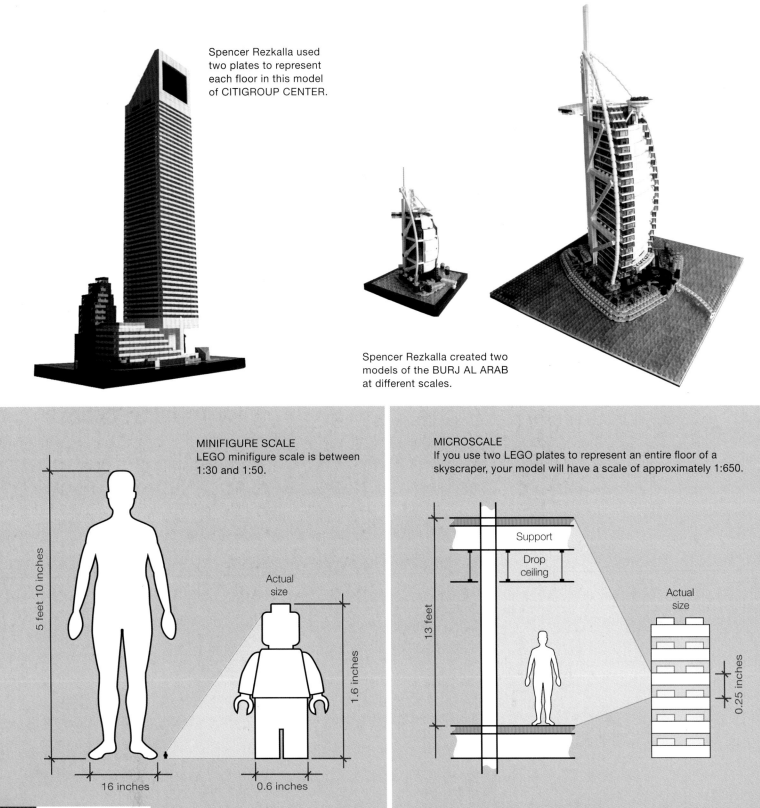

Spencer Rezkalla used two plates to represent each floor in this model of CITIGROUP CENTER.

Spencer Rezkalla created two models of the BURJ AL ARAB at different scales.

## MINIFIGURE SCALE

LEGO minifigure scale is between 1:30 and 1:50.

5 feet 10 inches

16 inches

Actual size

1.6 inches

0.6 inches

## MICROSCALE

If you use two LEGO plates to represent an entire floor of a skyscraper, your model will have a scale of approximately 1:650.

13 feet

Support

Drop ceiling

Actual size

0.25 inches

# SCALE

One key design tool for an architect is the scale model. The *scale* of a model describes how much smaller it is compared to the real building. Choosing the right scale for your LEGO model is a crucial first step.

## MINIFIGURE SCALE

Designing your model to fit a LEGO minifigure is one of the most popular approaches. Because LEGO minifigures are unrealistically short and wide, minifigure scale is not very precise, ranging from 1:30 to 1:50. An easy rule of thumb is to remember that a LEGO door is six bricks tall, so each floor of your model should be about eight bricks tall (about one foot per stud).

## MICROSCALE

When a LEGO architecture model is much too small for a LEGO minifigure to visit, this is called *microscale*. One approach to picking a scale is to decide how big you want your finished model to be, and calculate your scale with that goal in mind. This is how Adam Reed Tucker chose a scale of 1:200 when building his first large LEGO skyscraper. Adam wanted the model to be

at least eight feet tall so that viewers would have to look up to see it!

While some builders have a size in mind before they start building, others explore how to best capture the smaller details with LEGO and use that to determine the scale for the rest of the model. Spencer Rezkalla has built dozens of models based on the 1:650 scale, which "was the result of a fortunate accident when sizing my very first skyscraper model. At this scale, floor heights are reasonably modeled with one plate serving as a window and one as a spandrel [the panel between windows on different floors]." The 1:650 scale makes it possible to include every floor in a tall skyscraper by stacking alternating rows of clear and colored plates, as in Spencer's model of the Citigroup Center.

Building at larger scales requires a lot of bricks and space, but it can allow you to capture more details and more accurate proportions. When building his model of Wingspread, Jameson Gagnepain used an original blueprint of the house as the basis for his model: "I laid a grid over it using a photo editing program and used that to determine all scale wall lengths."

**BUILDER PROFILE:
J. SPENCER REZKALLA**

Spencer is a talented LEGO artist who has been building intricately detailed LEGO models for more than a decade. His fascination with tall buildings began when he was a young child growing up near New York City. He enjoys following the progress of new skyscrapers as they are being built, and sometimes completes a LEGO version before the actual building is finished.

By building all of his models at the same 1:650 scale, Spencer enables viewers to compare the sizes of famous buildings from around the world. This scale is large enough to capture the key details of each building without overwhelming the viewer. Each model is the result of extensive research into architectural theory, engineering, design, and the landmark's history. Spencer's work has been featured in books and magazines, displayed at museums, and re-created by fans around the world.

Spencer Rezkalla spends a lot of time on the space between his buildings, as in this model of the new WORLD TRADE CENTER.

Mattias Sondergaard placed his model of LOVELL HEALTH HOUSE in a lush landscape.

Adam Reed Tucker explores the form of FALLINGWATER in this model.

Jim Garrett included intricate Art Deco details in this model of the GUARDIAN BUILDING.

# FORM AND DETAIL

The LEGO artists featured in this book fall into two categories: those who focus on capturing the basic form of a building and those who prefer to create intricately detailed models. This stylistic difference is similar to how one painter prefers impressionism while another prefers realism.

## FORM

Adam Reed Tucker is most interested in capturing the "essence and pure sculptural form" in his LEGO models rather than perfect proportions and very fine details. Adam explains, "I view the LEGO brick as a creative medium, like paint to a painter or metal to a blacksmith." From his perspective, too much detail can make a LEGO model look more like a toy—a design philosophy that is clearly reflected in the models he designed for the official LEGO Architecture series and his large-scale models.

By focusing on the basic form, you can build a pretty large model using a small number of LEGO bricks. It can be liberating to stop worrying about the details and explore interesting shapes using basic bricks and simplified forms. Spencer Rezkalla relies on the "mind's eye" approach when designing the basic shape for his models—he builds "what you expect to see, rather than what's actually there, because landmarks are generally recognizable by the proportions of key architectural features."

When building very small models, you'll need to find creative ways to capture the essence of the building by eliminating unnecessary details.

## DETAIL

After capturing the basic form of a building, you can include some of its finer details. This is where specialty parts and advanced building techniques are helpful. Jameson Gagnepain explains the benefit of trial and error: "Getting the details right is all about refinement. I like to start with a rough picture by getting the lengths and colors right. I'll often revisit sections over and over again to improve them."

Context matters too! Spencer Rezkalla says, "Oftentimes, I spend more time designing plazas or an attached shopping center than I do with the main centerpiece tower." By placing your model in a landscape, you give it a sense of scale and make it easier for viewers to enjoy.

**BUILDER PROFILE: ADAM REED TUCKER**

As an architect and LEGO Certified Professional, Adam conceived and codeveloped the official LEGO Architecture series in 2008. He designed 15 iconic models in the series, including the White House, the Empire State Building, the Sydney Opera House, and Fallingwater. His proudest model in the series is the 2,276-piece model of Robie House. He also co-authored the book *LEGO Architecture: The Visual Guide* (DK, 2014).

Adam also builds LEGO models for public display, like the intricate model of Taliesin West featured on page 32. What gets Adam really excited are skyscrapers, which he prefers to build at a large scale to force viewers to look up, since "skyscrapers need to have a presence in order to command the respect they deserve."

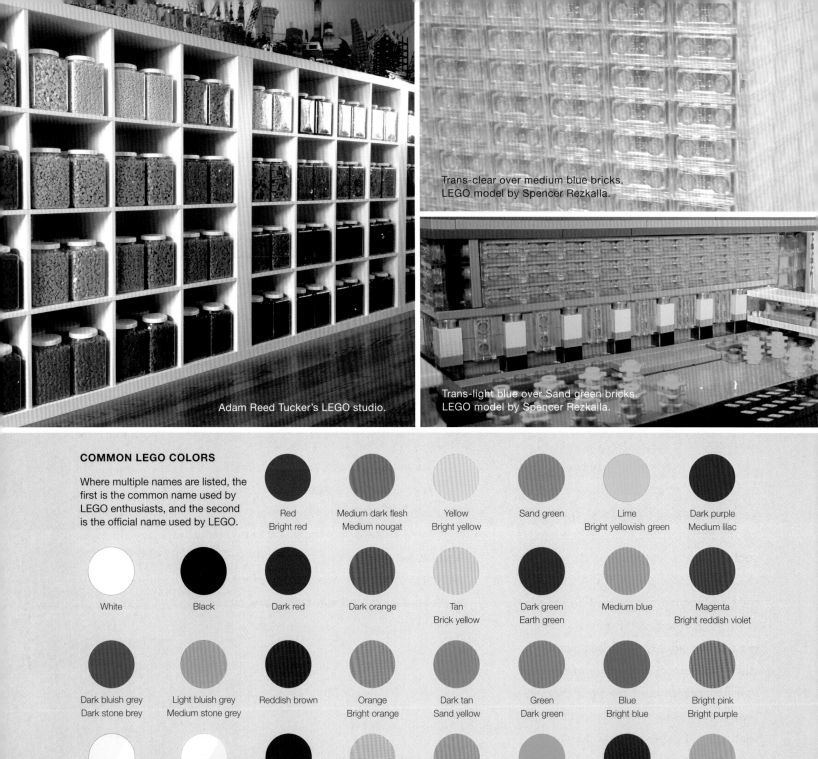

Trans-clear over medium blue bricks.
LEGO model by Spencer Rezkalla.

Trans-light blue over Sand green bricks.
LEGO model by Spencer Rezkalla.

Adam Reed Tucker's LEGO studio.

## COMMON LEGO COLORS

Where multiple names are listed, the first is the common name used by LEGO enthusiasts, and the second is the official name used by LEGO.

| | | |
|---|---|---|
| Red / Bright red | Medium dark flesh / Medium nougat | Yellow / Bright yellow |
| Sand green | Lime / Bright yellowish green | Dark purple / Medium lilac |

| | | | |
|---|---|---|---|
| White | Black | Dark red | Dark orange |
| Tan / Brick yellow | Dark green / Earth green | Medium blue | Magenta / Bright reddish violet |

| | | | |
|---|---|---|---|
| Dark bluish grey / Dark stone brey | Light bluish grey / Medium stone grey | Reddish brown | Orange / Bright orange |
| Dark tan / Sand yellow | Green / Dark green | Blue / Bright blue | Bright pink / Bright purple |

| | | | |
|---|---|---|---|
| Trans-clear | Trans-light blue | Dark brown | Bright light orange / Flame yellowish orange |
| Olive green | Bright green | Dark blue / Earth blue | Light pink / Light purple |

# COLOR

Although there are more colors in the LEGO universe than there were 20 years ago, there are still only about 30 colors to choose from. It's important to understand that not every part is available in every color—for example, there are more than 800 different LEGO parts currently available in black, 600 in white, and 125 in dark red but only 23 parts in sand green. A lack of parts in the color you need can feel like a big limitation when you're trying to create an accurate scale model.

Thankfully, you should be able to find the most common parts, like basic bricks, plates, tiles, and 1×1 cheese slopes, in almost every color. This gives you lots of choices when you're building walls or adding accents. For intricately detailed sections of your model, you will want to use the more common colors so you will have access to a broader selection of parts. Specialty parts and rare colors can be very expensive, as Jameson Gagnepain explains: "I very much wish that dark orange was more common. I've totally fallen in love with the color, and I wish the 1×1 plates weren't so rare."

## TRICKS WITH COLOR

Rather than fighting the limited palette of bright colors, Jonathan Grzywacz embraces the saturated colors when designing his modular buildings, which he describes as a kind of "Disney Main Street." In the same way that you might employ tricks of abstraction to re-create a complex form using LEGO bricks, you should feel free to embrace bright colors to give your model interest.

One of the cleverest tricks in working within this limited palette is using transparent parts on top of solid-colored bricks to achieve new colors. You can see examples on the facing page where Spencer Rezkalla used clear tiles on top of a medium blue brick to create a glass building with a faint blue glow, or trans-light blue with sand green under it to create the right color for his model of Taipei 101.

**BUILDER PROFILE:
ROCCO BUTTLIERE**

Rocco is a young LEGO artist with a passion for building intricate scale models of skyscrapers. His interest grew out of the LEGO Modular Buildings series and his "intrigue with the architecture of downtown Chicago." This led him to the Illinois Institute of Technology in Chicago, where he is studying architecture.

Rocco began building skyscrapers after seeing the work of Spencer Rezkalla at Brickworld 2008. He has since built more than 30 skyscrapers at the same 1:650 scale. Rocco is well on his way to achieving his ultimate dream—building an accurate scale model of downtown Chicago out of an estimated 3 million LEGO bricks.

Jumpers allow you to offset a wall by half of a stud.

Some parts have interesting textures.

Accessories can be used for accents, railings, or decorations.

Some bricks allow you to attach parts facing outward. This technique is called *studs not on top*, or *SNOT*.

Hinges, turntables, and clips allow you to work at any angle.

Technic parts allow you to build like an engineer.

Flexible tubing and clips allow you to create almost any shape.

# BRICKS

There have never been more ways to get the bricks you need to build amazing LEGO architecture models. The traditional approach is to buy LEGO sets that you find interesting, and use the parts from those sets to build your own creations. This can be a lot of fun, but architecture models typically need large numbers of the same parts, and most LEGO sets include only a few of each part.

The sets in the LEGO Architecture series naturally lend themselves to building your own models, as they contain a lot of small parts in the same color. The LEGO Architecture Studio set is also a great place to begin, because it contains 1,200 white and clear bricks. This allows you to experiment with a versatile selection of parts without worrying about matching colors.

Even if you have a large collection of bricks, you will eventually want to get more. You can buy directly from LEGO online or in LEGO retail stores, but the best option is to visit online stores where you can browse through every LEGO part that has ever been created, and see who has the parts you need available for purchase. You will find a list of great parts for building LEGO architecture models and advice on where to buy those parts at *http://nostarch.com/legoarchitect/*.

## ORGANIZING LEGO BRICKS

If you only have a small collection, you probably don't need to think much about organization. You can just dump all of the bricks on the floor and start building. However, as your collection grows, it can become frustrating to dig through a huge pile of LEGO bricks just to find a specific piece.

While it might seem like a good idea to sort your parts by color, it is very hard to find a specific red brick in a sea of other red bricks. I prefer to sort by category: bricks, plates, slopes, tiles, plants, minifigures, and the inevitable "miscellaneous" group. As your collection grows, you might want to sort further with separate containers for the different parts in each category, like 1×1, 1×2, and so on.

**BUILDER PROFILE: JARED CHAN**

Jared is a professional accountant living in Hong Kong, but it is easy to see that LEGO is his real passion. As with many other LEGO artists, Jared's enthusiasm for LEGO was redoubled when the Café Corner set was released in 2007.

Jared is very involved in the Legend Bricks Hong Kong LEGO Creators Club, where he has helped re-create iconic buildings in their city for public display. When creating a new model, he likes to visit the building and review design schematics if he can find them. His creations range from the large, intricate model of the HSBC Building featured on page 157 to the intimate minifigure-scale model of a typical 1970s public housing complex in Hong Kong, shown here.

# PHOTO CREDITS

## ARCHITECTURE PHOTOS

*Photographs courtesy Tom Alphin, except for those listed below.*

Air traffic control tower. Photo © **DELMAS LEHMAN** / Shutterstock.com.

Arc de Triomphe. Photo © **JEREMY REDDINGTON** / Shutterstock.com.

Bank of America Plaza. Photo © **CONNOR.CAREY**, used under CC BY-SA 3.0.

Barcelona Pavilion. Photo © **ASHLEY POMEROY** at en.wikipedia, used under CC BY-SA 3.0.

Bauhaus Dessau. Photo © **LELIKRON**, used under CC BY-SA 3.0.

Brandenburg Gate. Photo © **ELXENEIZE** / Shutterstock.com.

Burj Al Arab. Photo © **JOI ITO**, used under CC BY 2.0.

Centre Georges Pompidou. Photo © **CHARLES LEONARD** / Shutterstock.com.

Colony Hotel. Photo © **F11PHOTO** / Shutterstock.com.

Daily Express Building. Photo © **JAMIE BARRAS**.

Eames House. Photo © **EAMES OFFICE, LLC** (eamesoffice.com).

Empire State Building. Photo © **COCOZERO** / Shutterstock.com.

Engineering Research Center. Photo © **ROBERT A. FLISCHEL**.

Fallingwater. Photo by **CAROL M. HIGHSMITH**, Carol M. Highsmith's America, Library of Congress, Prints & Photographs Division.

Farnsworth House. Photo by **CAROL M. HIGHSMITH**, Carol M. Highsmith's America, Library of Congress, Prints & Photographs Division.

Gamble House. Photo by **CAROL M. HIGHSMITH**, Jon B. Lovelace Collection of California Photographs in Carol M. Highsmith's America Project, Library of Congress, Prints & Photographs Division.

Geisel Library. Photo © **FASTILY**, used under CC BY-SA 3.0.

Government Service Center. Photo by **MARC N. BELANGER**, public domain.

Guggenheim Museum Bilbao. Photo © **JONATAN ALONSO FERNANDEZ**.

Habitat 67. Photo by **NORA VASS**. © and stitched by **GERGELY VASS**, used under CC BY-SA 3.0.

Harold C. Bradley House. Photo © **BILL COLLINS**.

House in Katonah. Photo by **TOM BERNARD**. © Venturi, Scott Brown and Associates, Inc.

Imperial Hotel. Photo © **SANGAKU** / Shutterstock.com.

Jerry's Famous Deli. Photo © **JORG HACKEMANN** / Shutterstock.com.

Lake Shore Drive. Photo © **CHICAGO HISTORY MUSEUM**, HB-13809-L4, Hedrich-Blessing.

Lever House. Photo © **DAVID SHANKBONE**, used under CC BY-SA 3.0.

Michael Lee-Chin Crystal, Royal Ontario Museum. Photo © **ELLIOTT LEWIS**.

Miller House. Photo by **IK'S WORLD TRIP**, used under CC BY 2.0.

Monticello. Photo by **MARTIN FALBISONER**, used under CC BY-SA 3.0.

Neue Staatsgalerie. Photo © **CLAUDIO DIVIZIA** / Shutterstock.com.

Niagara Mohawk Building. Photo © **JEAN-PAUL RICHARD**, used under CC BY-SA 3.0.

Normal Theater. Photo © **KEN SMITH**.

Palace of Assembly. Photo © **J. PALYS** / Shutterstock.com.

Palácio do Planalto. Photo © **ANDRE DIB** / Shutterstock.com.

Phæno Science Center. Photo © **RICHARD BARTZ**, used under CC BY-SA 3.0.

Piazza d'Italia. Photo © **LOEWS NEW ORLEANS HOTEL**.

Quadracci Pavilion, Milwaukee Art Museum. Photo © **JOHN PICKEN**, used under CC BY 2.0.

Ransila I. Photo © **RÉMY STEINEGGER**.

Reggio Emilia AV Mediopadana. Photo © **STEFANO CARNEVALI** / Shutterstock.com.

Robarts Library. Photo by **CAZ ZYVATKAUSKAS**. © University of Toronto.

Robie House. Photo © **TEEMU08**, used under CC BY-SA 3.0.

The Rotunda, University of Virginia. Photo © **J. ADAM SOWERS**.

Royal Saltworks. Photo © **ALBAN MIRABAUD**.

Salk Institute. Photo by **CAROL M. HIGHSMITH**, Carol M. Highsmith Archive, Library of Congress, Prints & Photographs Division.

San Antonio Public Library. Photo by **LOURDES LEGORRETA**. © Legorreta + Legorreta.

Sony Tower. Photo © **DAVID SHANKBONE**, used under CC BY-SA 3.0.

Sydney Opera House. Photo © **DAVID ILIFF**, used under CC-BY-SA 3.0.

Taliesin III. Photo © **BILL HAMILTON**.

Taliesin West. Photo © **AARON REKER**.

Union Terminal. Photo © **DACOSLETT**, used under CC BY-SA 3.0.

Unité d'Habitation of Berlin. Photo © **CLAUDIO DIVIZIA** / Shutterstock.com.

United States Capitol Building. Photo © **MARTIN FALBISONER**, used under CC BY-SA 3.0.

Vanna Venturi House. Photo by **MATT WARGO**. © Venturi, Scott Brown and Associates, Inc.

Villa Emo. Photo © **BLAZ KURE** / Shutterstock.com.

Villa La Rotonda. Photo © **PIERGIORGIO MARTINI**.

Wainwright Building. Library of Congress, Prints & Photographs Division, HABS MO,96-SALU,49--4.

Walt Disney Concert Hall. Photo by **CAROL M. HIGHSMITH**. Carol M. Highsmith Archive, Library of Congress, Prints & Photographs Division.

White House. Photo © **ORHAN CAM** / Shutterstock.com.

William H. Emery Jr. House. Photo © **G LETOURNEAU**, used under CC BY-SA 3.0.

Willis Tower. Photo © **DANIEL SCHWEN**, used under CC BY-SA 4.0.

## LEGO PHOTOS

*All LEGO photographs are copyright of the individual builders, except for those listed below.*

The Acropolis. Photo courtesy of LEGO Certified Professional Ryan McNaught, thebrickman.com.

Colony Hotel. Photo courtesy of brickmania.com.

Taliesin West. Photo © **ANDREW PIELAGE**.

Transamerica Pyramid. Photo © **ANDREW BOSSI**.

Unité d'Habitation. Photo © **DEAN LAVENSON**.

Villa Hillcrest. Photo © **DEAN LAVENSON**.

*Further information about Creative Commons licenses may be found at the websites below.*

CC BY 2.0: *http://creativecommons.org/licenses/by/2.0/deed.en*

CC BY-SA 3.0: *http://creativecommons.org/licenses/by-sa/3.0/deed.en*

CC BY-SA 4.0: *http://creativecommons.org/licenses/by-sa/4.0/deed.en*

# BIBLIOGRAPHY

The text in this book is informed by a wealth of excellent books, documentary films, and online resources about architecture. This is just a short selection of the resources that had the greatest impact during my research.

Visit *http://nostarch.com/legoarchitect/* for a detailed bibliography with recommended reading, selected quotes, and more information about LEGO and architecture.

## BOOKS

DK Publishing. *Great Buildings*. London: DK, 2012.

Filler, Martin. *Makers of Modern Architecture: From Frank Lloyd Wright to Frank Gehry*. New York: New York Review Books, 2007.

—. *Makers of Modern Architecture, Volume II: From Le Corbusier to Rem Koolhaas*. New York: New York Review Books, 2013.

Glancey, Jonathan. *20th-century Architecture: The Structures That Shaped the Century*. New York: Overlook Press, 1998.

Gossel, Peter and Gabriele Leuthauser. *Architecture in the 20th Century*. Cologne: Taschen, 2012.

Hess, Alan and Alan Weintraub. *Frank Lloyd Wright Prairie Houses*. With contributions by Kathryn Smith. New York: Rizzoli, 2006.

Jencks, Charles. *The New Paradigm in Architecture: The Language of Postmodernism*. New Haven, CT: Yale University Press, 2002.

Legler, Dixie and Christian Korab. *Prairie Style: Houses and Gardens by Frank Lloyd Wright and the Prarie School*. New York: Stewart, Tabori and Chang, 1999.

Nichols, Karen, Lisa Burke, and Patrick Burke, eds. *Michael Graves: Buildings and Projects, 1990-1994*. With a foreword by Janet Abrams. New York: Rizzoli, 1995.

Palladio, Andrea. [1570]. *The Four Books of Architecture*. Translated by Isaac Ware. 1738. Reprinted with an introduction by Adolf K. Placzek. Mineola, NY: Dover Publications, 1965.

Pape, Thomas, Manfred Wundram, and Paolo Marton. *Palladio: The Complete Buildings*. 25th ed. Cologne: Taschen, 2008.

Poppeliers, John C., and S. Allen Chambers, Jr. *What Style Is It: A Guide to American Architecture*. Rev. ed. Hoboken: John Wiley & Sons, 2003.

Pryce, Will. *World Architecture: The Masterworks*. New York: Thames & Hudson, 2008.

Roeder, Annette. *13 Buildings Children Should Know*. Munich: Prestel, 2009.

Summerson, John. *The Architecture of the Eighteenth Century (World of Art)*. New York: Thames & Hudson, 1986.

Toman, Rolf, ed. *Neoclassicism and Romanticism: Architecture, Sculpture, Painting, Drawings: 1750-1848*. Potsdam: h. f. ullmann, 2008.

Venturi, Robert. *Complexity and Contradiction in Architecture*. New York: The Museum of Modern Art, 1966.

## FILMS

*Architectures*. Volumes 1-8. Directed by Stan Neumann, Richard Copans, et al. ARTE. 2007-2015.

*Bunkers, Brutalism and Bloodymindedness: Concrete Poetry with Jonathan Meades*. Parts 1 & 2. 118 minutes. Directed by Francis Hanly. BBC FOUR. 2014.

*Frank Lloyd Wright*. 146 minutes. Directed by Ken Burns and Lynn Novick. PBS. 1998.

*Oscar Niemeyer – A Vida É Um Sopro*. 90 minutes. Directed by Fabiano Maciel. 2010.

*Rococo: Travel, Pleasure, Madness*. Parts 1-3. 180 minutes. Directed by Waldemar Januszczak. BBC FOUR. 2014.

Safdie, Moshe. "Moshe Safdie on his iconic Habitat 67." *Dezeen* video, 2:40. December 19, 2014. *http://www .dezeen.com/2014/12/19/moshe-safdie-movie-interview -habitat-67/*

"Sketches of Frank Gehry," *American Masters*, season 20, episode 7. 83 minutes. Directed by Sydney Pollack. PBS. Aired September 27, 2006.

*Unfinished Spaces*. 86 minutes. Directed by Benjamin Murray and Alysa Nahmias. 2011.

## WEBSITES

Metropolitan Museum of Art. "The Grand Tour." *http:// www.metmuseum.org/toah/hd/grtr/hd_grtr.htm*.

Peeron. "Peeron Color List." *http://www.peeron.com/inv/ colors*.

New Elementary. "LEGO® colour chart reference." *http:// www.newelementary.com/2015/03/lego-colour-chart -reference.html*.

Wikipedia. "Architectural Style." Last modified April 14, 2015. *http://en.wikipedia.org/wiki/Architectural_style*.

# INDEX